THÉRÈSE

The Saint Who Loved Us

THÉRÈSE
The Saint Who Loved Us

A Personal View

Arthur Cavanaugh

Paulist Press
New York / Mahwah, N.J.

Acknowledgments

From *Story of a Soul,* translated by John Clarke, O.C.D. Copyright © 1975, 1976, 1996 by Washington Province of Discalced Carmelites, ICS Publications, 1231 Lincoln Road, N.E., Washington, D.C. 20002–1199 U.S.A.

From *St. Thérèse of Lisieux: Her Last Conversations,* translated by John Clarke, O.C.D. Copyright © 1977 by Washington Province of Discalced Carmelites, ICS Publications, 1231 Lincoln Road, N.E., Washington, D.C. 20002–1199 U.S.A.

From *General Correspondence: Volume One,* translated by John Clarke, O.C.D. Copyright © 1982 by Washington Province of Discalced Carmelites, ICS Publications, 1231 Lincoln Road, N.E., Washington, D.C. 20002–1199 U.S.A.

From *General Correspondence: Volume Two,* translated by John Clarke, O.C.D. Copyright © 1988 by Washington Province of Discalced Carmelites, ICS Publications, 1231 Lincoln Road, N.E., Washington, D.C. 20002-1199 U.S.A.

Jacket design by Trudi Gershenov
Book design by Lynn Else

Library of Congress Cataloging-in-Publication Data

Cavanaugh, Arthur.
    Thérèse : the saint who loved us : a personal view / Arthur Cavanaugh.
      p. cm.
    ISBN 0-8091-0570-5 (alk. paper)
    1. Thérèse, de Lisieux, Saint, 1873-1897. 2. Christian saints—France—Lisieux—Biography. 3. Lisieux (France)—Biography. I. Title.
    BX4700.T5 C35 2003
    282'.092—dc21

                                  2003004584

Published by Paulist Press
997 Macarthur Boulevard
Mahwah, New Jersey 07430 USA

www.paulistpress.com

Printed and bound in the United States of America

Contents

Author's Note

I wish to express my gratitude and my debt to Sandra Paterno for her valuable and faithful assistance in the preparation for many years of the manuscripts of my books.

Dedication

I dedicate this book, with love and thanksgiving,
to my two children, Teresa and Francis,
who have been the lights of my life.

The Statue in Church
1932

You may say of me that I lived,
not in this world, but in Heaven,
where my treasure was.

Early on, long before I came to write this book about her, St. Thérèse of Lisieux—the Little Flower, as she is equally known— was a figure of special interest to me, all because, at the age of eight, I'd discovered her statue in church one day and was immediately drawn to it. The impression the statue made on me might have passed away, to be forgotten, like so many flyaway impressions of mine at that age.

But it did not pass away, nor was it forgotten.

Saints are not given much notice in today's world. The adulation, the worship, is reserved for athletes, film stars and computer CEOs. In the world of the 1930s, my little patch of it in Woodhaven, Queens, New York, saints were enshrined as our heavenly heroes. At least, to me they were, a proper Catholic boy, of a family of Catholics on both sides for generations, and attending, of course, a Catholic school.

The lives of the saints were read to us by the sisters at school, and their virtues extolled. Holy cards imprinted with the images of saints were awarded as prizes in religion exams, models that we were to emulate. Although I'd often heard tell of these heroes, it wasn't until the encounter with the statue in church that a particular saint caught my attention.

The parish church reared up at the opposite corner from the yellow-brick school that I attended. One moment on that long-ago day, I was in the stampeding crowd of kids as school let out for the afternoon, and the next moment I'd pulled loose from the crowd and was headed down the block for the church.

I'm not sure of exactly why I sought out church that day. Given my load of troubles, I must have thought I could do with some extra praying to God for help.

I entered the church by way of the side door, which was closer than the front entrance around the corner. Well-trained by the sisters, I doffed my cap, dipped a finger in the holy-water font at the door, and crossed myself. Then, genuflecting before the altar, I went loping down the center aisle and slid into a pew halfway toward the rear, tipped my behind on the edge of the seat, and tossed my cap and schoolbag alongside me.

As I remember it, I was alone in the church that day. If some old ladies were lighting candles at the racks of vigil lights, or the stooped old sexton was shuffling around somewhere, I was oblivious of them and steeped in the quietness of empty pews as opposed to the crowds and shuffling feet at Sunday Mass. Such praying as I did was by rote, in sing-song unison with the class, Hail Marys and Our Fathers, but I sensed that was a different kind of prayer. I frowned in my effort to focus my mind on what I would say to God.

And nothing whatever, not a thought, not a word, not an aspiration took form in me.

The church, dim and chilling, gargoyles crouched atop the pillars, the lurid blood-red stained-glass windows, offered no inspiration to the eye. The statues of saints to be seen in the niches along the walls, a bearded, aged and infirm St. Joseph, a woeful and weeping St. Veronica, were forbidding creatures that did not invite the glance to linger or invoke the presence of God in the mind.

All true, but more than the church was causing my inability at prayer, and that was the low opinion I held of myself, very low, down in the cellar. It made any attempt to climb out of it seem doomed to failure. It had started, I reckoned, when I was three years old and was fitted with eyeglasses to correct my faulty squinting vision. I was not the same boy as before. The round discs of glass in the silver wire frame, like the eye-markings of a raccoon, marked me as defective and all-around inferior.

I shied away from the kids on the block and the taunts of "Four Eyes." I'd always felt loved by my parents, on an equal par with my brothers, but now I questioned it. I hung around close to the house, shut off from the life around me. "Listen here," I'd tell myself. "Don't be scared. Wait'll you get to school, and your life will change. You'll see, it'll be terrific."

But school, of course, was no different from before, shut off from the other children, unable to relate to them, the odd man out, presumed from my fumbling replies to sister's queries, to be stupid. By third grade, I'd stopped telling myself that my life would change. Nothing had changed, unless it was for the worse. Growing in me was the fear, gnawing in the gut, that unless I found some way out of the cellar of low opinion where I lived, I would be lost down there in the dark forever.

And what better way out of the cellar for me than God's help?

If I was nothing else, I was a Catholic, a believer in Jesus Christ, our Lord and Savior, who died on the cross out of love for us, to redeem us from our sins.

"Out of love"…and were I to pray to Jesus for help, would he not hear me?

I shifted my creaking legs on the kneeler and thought of a day last year, the rare and perfect day of my first communion, when deliverance from my troubles seemed imminent. I'd knelt at the altar rail, head tilted back, eyes closed, lips parted for the host the priest slipped onto my tongue, and then, swallowing it…what?

5

What then? A shaft of pure light, of Jesus coming into my soul, a moment of utter belief in him, that I was his child whom he loved.

Ah, yes, a moment of utter belief, but transitory, dissolving like wisps of smoke in the air, gone, like this moment now, the confidence leaking out of me.

I straightened up in the pew and fixed my gaze on the red sanctuary lamp on the altar, which signified that Jesus was present in the tabernacle, in the form of the Eucharist—isn't that what brought me to church?

Say it, Arthur...just three words, that's all..."Help me, Jesus"...say it!

No sound came from me, other than a ragged expulsion of breath. I leaned forward in the pew, nerves strained to breaking, but not a ghost of a prayer issued from my lips. I could not fight off the awful sense that, were I to pray to Jesus, he would not hear me, for why would he want to listen to someone like me?

I shoved up from the pew, angry, resentful at having wasted my time and effort. The afternoon light from the blood-red windows was dimming, and shadows were creeping over the rows of pews. The quicker I got out of this ugly church, the better I'd feel about it. I didn't bother to genuflect—why bother, it wouldn't matter to God—and went scuffing up the aisle. As I reached the doors to the vestibule, I caught a glimpse of a statue I had not noticed before, tucked in a niche at the rear of the side aisle.

It stood on a pedestal, half hidden in the shadows that obscured my view of it. Loathe to squander another wasted minute in church, nevertheless, I kept staring over the pews at the statue, and next I was standing back from it, hanging back in the side aisle.

The statue was of a young nun in a black veil and robes, her bare feet thrust in sandals. A white cloak was worn over the robes and hooked at the throat. Clasped in her arms was a crucifix abloom with red roses. The hint of a smile played on her fresh young face, and her head was inclined slightly toward me. It seemed as if her glance were directed at me, as mine was at her.

Since I had no idea who the statue represented, I moved up closer to it. The pedestal was at a level with my chin. I peered at the inscription at the base, below the sandaled feet: *St. Thérèse of Lisieux,* it read.

Some of my anger and resentment was appeased by the statue's gentle, smiling presence. I kept staring up at it, abuzz with questions. What were the funny accent marks that made a little roof over her name? Was Lisieux where she was from, and where was it? What had she done to make her a saint? It filtered into my mind, what the sister had told us, that saints were our friends in heaven, our emissaries to carry our prayers to God and obtain God's favors for us...*a friend in heaven*...might it apply to me, I wondered?

I felt that I wasn't looking at a statue but at the saint herself, in communion with her. Ah, if I were to ask her be my friend in heaven and obtain God's help for me, then maybe all of my troubles...

Oh, yeah, is that what you think? Well, answer me this: If God won't listen to you, why would a saint be any different?

I guessed it must be so, meaning that I'd have to struggle along on my own steam, minus any help from above. That's how it was for me.

I threw the statue a last, lingering look, turned heel, and exited from the church, finished and done with prayer, though apparently not with a certain saint.

As I steered up one Woodhaven street and down another, the image of a young nun, a crucifix of roses in her arms, floated above, like a banner in the sky, following after me, all the way home.

The encounter in church had made a dazzling impression on me. For days afterward, I went over and over the encounter in my mind. A special presence had come into my life, in the form of a statue. Saints were suppose to strike awe in us, remote and unapproachable, but that's not how it was with this saint. I felt intimately at home with her, as if we were related and I were her kid brother. I think I must have loved her straight off. She was my saint, *my* Thérèse, though I knew nothing of her or what had made her a saint.

This love of a saint was a direct contradiction of my increasing disaffection for the religion in which I'd been reared. Since I was unworthy of God's help, what was I doing at Mass every Sunday and on my knees by my bed every night? More and more, over the next few years, I took to associating my unhappiness, my difficulties, with being a Catholic, and I wanted to get as far away from it as I could.

Strangely enough, I didn't associate my saint with the disavowal of my faith. I held her separate and apart from it, but it's true that, after I'd left home for college and ceased altogether the practices of a Catholic, the image of Thérèse, once so radiant, grew ever dimmer in my recollection of her.

So it was therefore to my astonishment that as a young man, years later, I should chance upon a second encounter, more dazzling than the first, with the never-forgotten saint of my childhood.

It happened in Paris. in March 1945, during World War II. I'd been overseas for six months, an actor in the U.S.O. Camp Shows production of a Broadway comedy, *Junior Miss*. We were touring the Army bases up and down the length of France, giving performances for the troops. That winter was of record freezing temperatures and snows in France. No way out of the cold, no heat in the hotels and inns where we were billeted, no heat in the trailer-truck in which we traveled over the icy, rutted roads. My chronic sniffles had turned to pneumonia and a week of delirium and massive antibiotics in an Army hospital in Marseilles. Unable to go on with the tour, weak and undernourished, thin as a rail, I was sent to Camp Shows headquarters outside Paris to await Army travel orders to ship me home. Since no civilian trains were running, Camp Shows provided a jitney for transport each morning into the city, and back again to headquarters at night.

It was on one of these outings into Paris that the encounter occurred. It was nothing that I'd sought, indeed, would have gone out of my way to avoid. This time it wasn't with a statue of St. Thérèse, but with something precious belonging to her. Later I would learn it was what she did with her entire life, she gave it away, her very self freely, of her own account.

Out of love...

As I'd been doing all week, I hopped off the jitney at the Étoile, that morning early in March 1945. The jitney tooled off down the long, wide, mist-hung sweep of the Champs Élysee, while I squatted down on a nearby bench, like a wearied old man with shaky legs. It's approximately how I felt, old and tired and worn out, emotionally decimated by what I'd see of the carnage and destitution of war. I scarcely knew who I was anymore. I'd lost who I was, my true self, long ago...

Home!

Never before in my life had I yearned so desperately for my home and family. Yet, even as I yearned for it, squatted on this bench in the chill mists of Paris, not caring how I spent the day, just so that it would pass quickly into night—another part of me was uncaring of the prospect of home. What was my future to be? It was like looking at a movie screen gone blank. A career as an actor no longer held any thrill for me. Earlier, I'd wanted to be a writer, but that seemed equally beyond my ken.

I'd lost my way, that's the gist of it, not just from the war, but a long time ago, as a little boy, stumbling along blindly ever since, without any meaning to my life…

I pushed up from the bench in the Étoile, flailing my arms and stamping my feet from the cold. Unless I intended to squander the rest of the day in idle misery, I'd better hatch some idea of where to spend it more profitably.

Paris in wartime was not the glittering pleasure dome of legendary reputation. The museums were closed, except for special days, and the shops, with few wares to sell, were shuttered by afternoon, the restaurants open for a few hours in the evening, until the supply of food ran out. Wherever I'd ventured, the wet, damp, misty cold was my companion, indoors as well as out, in a critical shortage of fuel. It was a trifling hardship compared to the rigors the war had imposed on the people of Paris. They were everywhere to be seen, the crippled soldiers on crutches in patched-up uniforms, the famished children in rags, begging candy bars from the G.I.s. Everywhere were the women of Paris, old and young, thin and ghostly, garbed in threadbare black, as they shuttled in the icy cold from one market stall and butcher shop to the next, in the tenuous hope of snaring a baguette of bread, a bunch of carrots or onions or potatoes, a scrap of meat or meat bones, to provide supper that night on the family table.

A city's deprivations at least had the effect of prodding me from my lethargy. I pulled from my trenchcoat pocket a dog-eared Michelin travel guide of Paris. I flipped the pages to a map of the

Metro subway system and raised a finger over the map, ready to plunge down at it.

Since I was physically unable to explore the city by foot, I'd devised this method of picking where by subway I'd go, at whatever station my finger landed the nearest to.

Down went my punching finger upon the map.

Chatelet was the Metro station nearest to my finger.

Very well, that's where I'd take myself today, to see what I would see, feast or famine, who knows which it would be?

So then, with that decided, I trooped down the stairs of the Étoile Metro and stepped onto a train that went roaring in and out of the stations. I kept an eye out for the stop to get off at and felt my spirits on an upswing. I was going somewhere, if only at the bidding of my finger, and not still squatted like a tired old man on a bench.

Place du Chatelet stood across the boulevard from the river embankment. The magnificent fountain spouted no geysers of water, shut off by the war. The huge sprawl of the Louvre could be glimpsed in the misty distance, and beyond it the budding springtime green of the Tuileries. The war had robbed Paris of its glitter and luxuries but had given it a somber, austere beauty of another kind.

The district's array of municipal buildings wasn't of interest to me. My attention kept straying over to the embankment, the bridge that crossed over the Seine to the ancient Ile de la Cité. The tiny isle, less than a mile in diameter, was dwarfed by the soaring gothic bell towers and enormous girth of Notre Dame Cathedral, but that didn't interest me, either.

However, by consulting the Michelin, I saw that I could cross over from the Cité to the Left Bank, the bookstalls, the cafes, the Latin Quarter, which interested me a great deal more.

So that's what I did. I ventured over the bridge to the Cité, on a day that would leave a profound impression on me, the beginning of the changes in my life.

Guided by a map of the Cité in the Michelin, I headed for the square of Notre Dame. From there, I would reach the bridge over to the Left Bank. Except that I couldn't quite get to the square. I saw with annoyance that it was closed from access by a ring of police sawhorses, and by the crowds held back by the sawhorses.

The crowds were composed primarily of women, of every age and class, rich and poor, some with children and babes in arm. Nuns in white-winged coifs, priests in flat round hats and black tunics, and crippled soldiers hobbling on crutches completed the assembly. Rather than exhibiting a festive holiday spirit, these citizens of Paris were quiet and subdued, as if they were gathered to witness some sort of religious event to be staged in the square.

A religious event…such as what, for instance? Well, perhaps it was a holy day, observed in France, but not in the States. Or it might be the feast day of a saint much venerated in France, if not elsewhere in the world. It suddenly occurred to me, as it had not until then, that the country in which I'd lived for almost six months was a nation primarily of Catholics, and of a church established for centuries.

Penned in by the crowd on my side of the square, I glanced above the rooftops at a soaring symbol of the church in France, thrusting up at the sky. From the immense carved gothic-arched portals in front, to the medieval splendor of the Rose Window, set between the bell towers, high above, to the sculpted stone figures of kings and saints, angels and prophets, that adorned every inch, every pediment and abutment of the facade, the Cathedral of Notre

Dame invoked the power and awe that a great work of art inspires in the viewer.

Ah, yes, but not in me. I didn't ask, didn't seek, didn't want to be here, detained, thwarted by the sawhorses. I wanted to push and shove my way out of here, away from the crowds of the faithful. Once, oh, years ago, as a boy, I might have belonged among them, but that was long ago, before I'd discarded my faith.

Still, like it or not, I was stuck here, no getting out of it.

From the cathedral, mighty chords of organ music washed over the square, and a wave of excitement swept through the crowds. The event, the occasion, whatever it was, so patiently waited for, was about to take place in the square. To the joyous ringing, reverberating clamor of the tower bells, the great cathedral's portals, the royal entrance of kings, slowly were parting...

What had become of the boy I once was? How had he grown to be me, sick of spirit, still nursing old hurts, old wounds, disconsolate, lost and bereft, belonging nowhere, to nothing at all?

A procession emerged upon the cathedral steps, to the cries and exclamations of the crowds. All around me, the sign of the cross was traced on brows and breasts. Was it a holy day, or a feast day? What was the occasion for it? Down the steps and along the other side of the square went the procession, two by two, altar boys, incense wafting from their censers, monks in brown robes, nuns in white cloaks and black veils, priests in vestments...

The unhappy, troubled boy, kneeling one afternoon in church, in need of help. Of a low self-esteem, he wasn't able to ask help from God. Nor could he ask it of the saint whose statue he'd spied in the church, of a young smiling nun, her arms heaped with roses, that had so entranced him. No, he couldn't pray to her for help. If God wouldn't listen to him, why would she?

But what if the boy were mistaken in his thinking? A prayer was a prayer, after all. Silent or not, unspoken or not, wasn't it still a prayer, and wasn't God entirely capable of hearing it?

I noticed, as I watched the procession, that at the rear of the long advancing line a golden silk canopy was raised above a...a *what?* It looked to be a casket, of all unimagined things! Diminutive in size, it was carried aloft on the shoulders of four priests in robes, but that wasn't the only startling aspect of the scene. At the casket's approach, women, one after another, would break from the sawhorses to hurl flowers at it, some to kneel in mute appeal, hands clasped in supplication, as the casket was borne past them.

Mystified, though I was, it dawned on me that, while the ceremonies might entail some other significance, the procession was to honor, in the casket, the relics of a saint. By then, as the long line wound on, the square was scattered with roses in tribute to that saint.

The roses, the roses!

It would certainly be more dramatic to report that as the casket was carried along my side of the square, I impulsively pushed forward in the crowd, busting loose from the sawhorses, to raise a hand to touch the casket, the relics of a saint.

Who was it, who could it be other than my Thérèse?

I stayed where I was, however, hemmed in by the crowd, too stunned to do anything but to wonder dumbly at my presence in the square. I didn't choose, didn't want to be here, yet here was exactly where I was. A prayer was a prayer, spoken or not. If my long-ago prayer for help was heard, who would have heard it, if not the saint I'd called mine? And was it beyond the limits of credulity to consider that it was she, who, by the punch of my finger on the Metro map, had fetched me here?

Ah, sure, I shrugged it off, that's exactly what a Catholic would say...and in a blinding flash I realized that, all along, a Catholic is what I'd been.

And, perhaps, in these years when I'd felt myself to be alone and lost, I was never really that at all.

I lingered there in the square, long after the procession had returned to the cathedral and the crowds had dispersed. The occasion for the ceremonies, other than to honor the relics of a saint, was still a puzzle to me. I stood there in the gray mists and the sharp bite of wind from the river, the magnificence of the cathedral towering above me, while I pondered the tumult of emotions the day had aroused in me, and the course that seemed indicated for me to follow. Already, a newfound sense of resolve was stirring in me to set my life on a different course.

With that, I turned away from the deserted square and crossed back over the bridge to the Chatelet Metro, thinking of the saint who this day had burst into my life, whose own life I knew nothing of.

The puzzle of the ceremonies in the square was answered for me two days later.

I'd met, sharing a lunch table at the Officers' Mess, an Army chaplain who was devoted to St. Thérèse and had been in the crowds at the procession. As he told it to me, the mortal remains of the saint had reposed in the basilica erected in homage to her in Lisieux, a shrine visited each year by thousands of pilgrims. But then, in 1944, when plans were finalized for the Allied invasion of Normandy, the bloody assault on Omaha Beach, it was feared by church officials that the massive bombing of the surrounding countryside might destroy the basilica in Lisieux and with it the precious relics of a saint, who, incidentally, had been declared with Joan of Arc to be patron and protector of France. The decision was made to remove the relics from the basilica and to take them to Paris to be safeguarded in the vaults of Notre Dame, until such time as the reliquary could be returned to Lisieux.

The ceremonies I'd witnessed two days before were to commemorate the homeward journey, later that day, of the relics to Lisieux. Although the bombing had devastated the town itself, the basilica was left untouched. It has prompted some, including the chaplain who gave me the story, to attribute the sparing to another of the saint's miracles.

It was the first, but by no means the last, of what I would learn, eventually by years of research, of the many-faceted story of St. Thérèse. Here again in these pages, her story is told, from a personal view of the subject, not of a pious and pretty doll-house saint, but of a vibrant, flesh-and-blood, living-and-breathing young woman embarked on an epic spiritual journey, bold and daring, exploring new frontiers of God's love and merciful forgiveness that would radically alter the thinking and attitudes of her church.

As the author of some novels and short stories, I had no experience with biography when I began this book. It has been a labor of many wrong turns and revisions, but that ultimately shed light on the character of my subject. I hope that for those who know little or nothing about Thérèse, my book will shed a similar light upon her life and her mission.

PART ONE

Death of a Nun
1897

God gave me courage in proportion
to my sufferings, but I am not afraid,
since if they increase, He will increase
my courage at the same time.

1.

In 1897, more than a hundred years ago, a young Carmelite nun, hidden away from the world in a monastery in Normandy, in northern France, died of tuberculosis. She was twenty-four years old, and her existence beyond the narrow, restricted confines of her life was entirely unknown.

Unknown, but as it turned out, not for long.

In 1925, just twenty-eight years later, glittering ceremonies were held in St. Peter's in Rome for the canonization of Thérèse Martin, of the monastery in Lisieux, France. The swiftness of her canonization was unprecedented in the history of the church, as was the international coverage of the event by the press.

Until the recent reforms of Pope John Paul II, the act of canonization was a slow and cautious, snail-like and frequently stalled procedure. A court of law was set up, in effect, for and against the defendant. The reams of documents pertaining to the candidate were scrutinized, the evidence pro and con was heard again and again, exhaustively. The process could and did last for centuries. Joan of Arc, to cite one example, who died in 1531, burned as a witch at the stake in Rouen, was not declared a saint of the church until 1920, four years before Thérèse was honored.

It could be said, moreover, that Thérèse's canonization was the outcome, less of procedure, than of a public outcry throughout the world for it. The means by which this was accomplished was a book that, mysteriously, Thérèse had never intended to write, never finished, and until the last days of her life, gave no thought to its publication. It was a book, the recollections of a nun, so unlikely to garner the world's attention that the idea of it happening might be compared to the fantasy of the Victorian age of rocketing a man to the moon.

And, to compound the mystery, the completion and publication of the book was occasioned only by the author's death.

In the hidden life of Thérèse in the monastery, a book was the last thing that would have been expected of her. Not much, indeed, was expected of her by the nuns of her community in the nine years of her tenure among them...

It was the custom in Carmel, upon the death of a nun, to send an obituary of her life to the other houses of the order, in this instance, in France, but that in itself posed a problem. The nuns of the Lisieux Carmel were of decidedly mixed opinions in regard to Sister Thérèse, before and after her eyes had closed in death. What of merit, as one of the nuns was heard to ask, could be claimed for her? A good little soul, to be sure, but of no particular achievement, and in some cases, quite the reverse.

She had been a slow if conscientious worker in her duties in the refectory, the sacristy, the linen room. Incompetent was the word for her housekeeping skills. She had dabbled inconsequently in painting and poetry, of no practical value in a community dependent on its labors for income. Who had not observed Thérèse nodding off to sleep at night prayers in the chapel? Worse, her extreme youth, fifteen when she'd entered Carmel, and her childish demeanor had made her the spoiled pet of the prioress; thus she was spared the rod of discipline. The list of deficiencies went on, some of which were true and others the antithesis of truth.

A question mark against her character was that Sister Thérèse had failed to qualify as a chapter nun, that is, given a seat on the governing council of the Carmel, and with it a vote every three years in the election of the prioress. Relegated to the low rank of novice, she had nevertheless been assigned to the instruction of the novices. It was still another example of the prioress's favoritism, although, in fairness, Thérèse had shown a certain aptitude in that capacity.

No, really, to summarize the opinion of many of the nuns, what could be claimed in the obituary of someone whose presence had to a large degree passed unnoticed by the community? A good little soul, but that's about it. Well, death would bring a closure to her life, and that would be the end of it. Admittedly, there were those in the community who did not agree with this negative estimate of the deceased, and who were of quite a different opinion of Sister Thérèse. Ah, well, time, as always, would tell which estimate was true and which was false.

A different opinion was woefully inadequate to describe the contrary belief held by a faction of nuns in the monastery. Absolute was their conviction, beyond any doubt or swaying, that a saint had dwelled side by side with them in the cloister, one whose hidden life of sanctity, seemingly so ordinary, had made of her a saint.

But now, with the death of Sister Thérèse, a life cut short long before its prime, the chances of advancing the cause of a saint appeared to be doomed to everlasting failure...

The leader of this grieving and passionate band of advocates was uniquely equipped to be its postulator. Mother Agnes of Jesus—the title was hers from a term of office as prioress—was one of Thérèse's three siblings who had shared her life in the Carmel. Not only that, Agnes had enjoyed a relationship with her forged by more than the ties of blood. Older by sixteen years, she had served, from the beginning, as teacher, counselor and mentor to the youngest of the Martin sisters, still thought of perpetually as "the baby." By this endearment Thérèse often signed the notes to her sisters. After the death of their mother, when Thérèse was four, Agnes had become her chosen mother, deepening the bond between them. Although once in Carmel, Thérèse had charted her own course as a nun, Agnes had continued to offer herself as teacher and counselor. She had watched her protégée's daily gains and setbacks in her vocation, sometimes harshly critical of her, ready with advice not always taken, supremely confident of her potential for spiritual growth. From childhood on, Thérèse had expressed a determination to become a saint, but that, of course, was a distant, far-off goal.

Yet perhaps that goal was not too distant, Agnes would discover, in a burst of revelation that would transform her into the postulator of a saint's cause.

With the approaching death of Thérèse, a sorrowing band of believers in the cause had formed around Mother Agnes. The group was composed of her two other sisters, no less devoted to their dying sibling. It included a cousin, a fifth of the family to enter the Carmel, and two or three novices, starry-eyed with admiration and love for their former instructress. Moreover, all believed with equal passion that they held the evidence, the incontestable proof, to support their claim.

And what was the evidence?

It consisted of a handful of manuscripts from the pen of Thérèse, two schoolgirl copybooks filled with her script, and a sheaf of notepaper, the last from her pen. If left to her own inclinations, none of the manuscripts would have existed. Initially, Thérèse wrote a memoir at the command of Agnes, her prioress at the time.

It was this memoir, when at length she read it, that had so transformed Agnes into the postulator of a cause.

At first glance, the memoir, written at odd hours, usually late at night, in fatigue, with numerous errors in grammar and spelling, left uncorrected, was of dubious merit. Ah, but one had only to sample the pages, Agnes would exclaim to herself, to be struck by lightning. Here in these confiding pages was a hidden life of the spirit that, revealed, glowed like a jewel. So unutterably moved by what she had read, Agnes was resolved that Thérèse must continue to write of the glory that was hidden in the very ordinariness of her life. No longer the prioress, able to issue commands, Agnes sought and obtained a command from the reigning prioress, by which Thérèse had completed a second copybook of memories. And last were the sheets of notepaper, composed while she lay dying in the infirmary, ending in a faltering pencil that trailed off the paper, unfinished...

Unfinished... was that to be the fate of the manuscripts? A life cut short, unfinished, that, too? Surely not, yet who in the Carmel, other than the believers, would protest such a verdict?

The cause was doomed.

The monastery bells tolled the mournful announcement. The death watch was over, moments ago. A final "Te Deum," and the community of nuns, veils lowered, filed slowly out of the infirmary, to the tolling of the bells. Thérèse still lay in the bed where death had mercifully overtaken her, raised up on the pillows, alone and unattended.

The arrangements for her funeral and burial must be made. Charged with the task was Agnes, who was inconsolable with grief and incapable at the moment of proceeding with it.

Agnes's grief was that of a mother at the loss of her child. For three interminable months, in tandem with her two sisters, she had served as nurse to Thérèse, witness to the agonies inflicted by a death from tuberculosis. Even then, Agnes and her sisters had jotted on scraps of paper the patient's conversations with them, to be preserved in notebooks for further use...or would there be any use for them?

The obituary must be prepared and sent out, but Agnes shrank from that task in her grief. What was to be done with the manuscripts, much in need of editing, and in no condition for publication? Well, perhaps the idea was nothing more than a dream expired, like the writer herself.

Agnes's lost child lay waiting to be readied for her coffin. As she stood grieving at the bed, did Agnes ask herself if it had all been in vain? How had a cause so right and just come to naught? Her thoughts surely traveled back to the beginning, to the house in Alençon, in which a family had awaited with joy as well as trepidation the birth of this very child...

2.

"I love children, even to the point of folly, and I was born to have them for my own," wrote Zélie Martin in a letter to her sister and frequent correspondent, Sister Dosithée, a nun in the Visitation convent in Le Mans. It was the winter of 1872, and Zélie's home in Alençon was a beehive of activity, domestic and otherwise. Uppermost in her thoughts, however, was the approaching birth of her ninth child and the anxieties that accompanied it.

The role of wife and mother over which she rejoiced was at variance with Zélie's earlier ambitions. As a young girl, she had applied for admission to the Sisters of Charity of St. Vincent de Paul in Alençon and had been summarily refused, a crushing disappointment, but Zélie wasn't one to cry over spilt milk. She accepted the refusal as God's will for her, as she would accept all of life's reversals, and set to the task of earning her livelihood. Since few other options were available for women, she taught herself the art of lace-making. The provincial town of Alençon in Normandy was celebrated for its lace, the exquisite Pointe d'Alençon that fetched exorbitant prices in the luxury shops of Europe and America. It would prove a wise and lucrative choice for Zélie.

Not content with making lace, she organized a cooperative of women in the trade, sketched the patterns, supervised the delicate, tortuous needlework, paid the women, and negotiated the sale of the lace with the visiting agents who represented the shops. It wasn't long before Zélie's account ledger showed a tidy profit, but was that, she implored her God at daily Mass, to be her life? It is likely that, with typical French practicality, she viewed her profits as a means of acquiring a dowry with which to contract for a marriage.

So it was that, in 1858, Zélie Guérin was introduced to a townsman, the proprietor of a jewelry shop, the shy, reticent, thirty-five-year-old Louis Martin. He, too, had aspired to a life in religion. The young Louis, inclined to dreamy solitude, had presented himself as a candidate at the fabled Monastery of the Great St. Bernard in the Swiss Alps, whose monks were dedicated to the rescue by sleds and dogs of mountain climbers lost in the snowy vastness. Louis, too, was refused admission, just as Zélie had been. It is doubtful, when the two met, that Louis contemplated marriage. A watchmaker, he'd lived for years a semi-monastic life of daily Mass and retirement from the world, while attending to the customers of his jewelry shop.

But Zélie was to change his life.

Unfortunately, owing to the fame of one of their daughters, Zélie and Louis have been made by pious hagiographers into plaster images, complete with haloes and minus a blemish or defect, denied the hard reality and complexities of their actual lives. When, in 1858, the couple was married in the Church of Notre Dame in Alençon, it was emphatically not a union of romantic love. A practicing celibate, Louis's idea of marriage was for them to live in mutual celibacy, as brother and sister. Informed of this, Zélie complied with his dictum…until she'd talked him out of it. Children, she protested, were the precious fruit of marriage, children to offer to God's service as priests and nuns. Always to her, mistakenly, there was a higher calling than her own exemplary one.

The newlyweds settled into a rented house on the Rue de Pont Neuf in Alençon. Over the next fourteen years, while Zélie's lace business prospered to the extent that Louis sold the jewelry shop to become her partner in the flourishing enterprise, the Martins became the parents of eight children, who were both the abiding joy and sorrow of Zélie's busy, overworked life.

Which takes us again to the winter of 1872 and Zélie's letter to Sister Dosithée, in anticipation of the birth of her ninth child. By then, the family had moved to a larger house on the Rue St. Blaise, which Louis had inherited on his father's death. If fear was mingled with Zélie's joy at the approaching birth, there was reason for it. Of the Martins' eight children, four had died, two boys and two girls, in infancy, except for Hélène, who had lived to the age of five. Of the four survivors, all were girls—Marie, the eldest, followed by Pauline, Léonie and Céline. All would play important roles in our story.

It is interesting, indeed, astonishing, in view of the future, to quote from a letter Sister Dosithée wrote to Zélie in 1870, to console her for the loss of Hélène, mindful as she was of her sister's desire to give her children into the service of the Lord.

"That faith and confidence of yours which never wavers will one day have their reward," Sister Dosithée predicted. "For won't you be well recompensed if God, well pleased with you, gives you the great saint which, for His Glory, you have wanted?"

As the days of December went by, the time for the baby's delivery was imminent. But then, with Christmas come and gone, the delivery, in Zélie's calculations, was overdue and cause for fresh alarm. Zélie was forty-one and nearing the end of her childbearing years. What if the baby in her womb were the last she would conceive? Oh, how she had loved each of her eight children and would ever grieve for the loss of the four. She'd already chosen a name for the baby, in memory of Mélanie-Thérèse, the last to die. Was that perhaps tempting fate? And what if the delay in the delivery were a sign that she must again endure the loss of her baby?

Of Zélie fears, there was one she kept to herself and dared not dwell on. As a girl, she had injured her left breast. A tumorous lump had formed, benign, but capable, the doctors warned, of metastasizing into cancer. She would not, could not, as the mother of four girls in need of her, give credence to that dread possibility.

If Zélie was increasingly the prey of fears, she did what she always did in dealing with them. She persevered in her busy routine of work and mothering. She endured her fears as stoically and courageously as she had lived her life.

The delivery held off until after the advent of the New Year. In a surge of gratitude and relief, she wrote from her bed to her brother, Isidore Guérin, who owned a pharmacy in Lisieux. "My little daughter was born yesterday [January 2] at eleven-thirty that night. She seems very nice, and what I experienced before [the loss of the four] is not to be counted."

So was announced the birth of the Martins' ninth child. The baby was christened Marie Francoise Thérèse in the parish church, and her name, which the world would celebrate, was recorded in the long anonymous columns of names in the church registry.

Within days of her birth, in the ordinary course of life's tribulations, the baby's health deteriorated, and within weeks, to the despair but not the surrender of her mother, the tiny, frail bundle of life hovered near death.

The baby, Thérèse, was diarrhetic, unable to retain nourishment. To compound the crisis, her one source of nourishment, the milk of her mother's breasts, had dried up. She could not stomach the substitute formulas prescribed by the doctor. Aghast at her baby's precipitous decline, the skeletal form, the sickly pallor, Zélie was frantic but not ready to concede defeat. She initiated a search in the town for a wet nurse. It was no guarantee of success, for the baby might as quickly reject as accept the nurse's milk, and that would consign her, like the four lost ones, to the grave.

The Martin family shared the mother's desperation. The baby in her crisis had become precious to all of them. A farm woman, Rose Taillé, was recommended to Zélie as a person of Christian virtue and robust vigor. Wasting not an hour of time, Zélie hired a wagon and horse and drove the eight kilometers to the woman's farm in Semallé. At first Rose refused to leave her home and children, but struck by Zélie's anguished pleas, she consented to a week's trial in Alençon, and the two women set off in the wagon for town.

As soon as they reached the house, the dying baby was given Rose's breast and the family crowded around her. In a very few minutes Thérèse was sucking hungrily at the milk, which afterward she did not reject.

She had survived the crisis, at least for the moment. At the week's conclusion, Zélie was left with no alternative but to hand over her baby to Rose Taillé. Thérèse accompanied her in the wagon back to the farm in Semallé, where, in reviving health and spirits, she remained for a year.

Zélie, deprived of her baby, often visited the farm, sometimes with the other girls in tow. From another of her letters, we are given a delightful snapshot of Thérèse in a rustic setting of barnyard chicks and hens, "brown as a berry and lying in a nest of hay in a wheelbarrow." She would be carted to the fields and tethered in Rose's apron on the back of a cow to await her nursing time. By the year's end, rosy-cheeked, golden-haired, buoyant with health, Thérèse returned home to her family. It was a banner day for the Martins. The child, plucked from the jaws of death, had by God's will been restored to them, was doubly precious to them, and was from then on the family's petted darling.

And thus began for Thérèse what she would later designate as the first of the three periods of her childhood, which, by its finish, would impose on her happiness a heavy penalty.

3.

What is meant by saying that the Martins were an ordinary family? In the 1870s, families like them were to be found in every town and city of France, hard-working, thrifty, practical, Victorian in outlook, staunchly Catholic, as much for the social as the religious distinction, and dedicated above other considerations to the care of the home and family unit as supreme and sacrosanct.

The Martins shared all of these characteristics except that the practice of their religious convictions was profound. There was also the fact that one of them was a genius, whose accomplishments would set the family forever apart by hagiographers, endowing them with virtues that ignored or dissembled their very real humanity.

Thérèse, of course, wrote of her family, but perhaps a richer source of information is a collection of family letters, never intended for publication, and thus the more revealing. The telephone, invented in 1876, was not made a state service in France until 1899. There, as elsewhere, people separated by distances depended on pen and paper and the mail to communicate with one another. Letters, sent and received, were preserved as keepsakes, copied out to be forwarded to other parties, but scrupulously preserved as a chronicle of births and deaths, weddings and celebrations, and life's everyday events.

The family letters, especially those of Zélie, that tireless correspondent, provide us with an intimate picture of the daily ebb and flow of life as the Martins experienced it, minus the embellishments that would later enshrine them.

So, then, let us visit the house at 36 Rue St. Blaise in Alençon. The year is 1877, when the youngest of the family, the petted darling, is four and will learn before the year's end that where there is sunshine, also, immutably, there are shadows.

A painted sign above the door of the house was inscribed *Louis Martin, Fabricant Pointe d'Alençon*. The success of Zélie's lace business had raised the couple from the merchant class to that of the bourgeoisie. They were able to afford servants for the household chores and to send the two oldest girls, Marie and Pauline, to the

Visitation convent boarding school in Le Mans, where Aunt Dosithée kept a fond eye on them. By 1877, while Pauline, at sixteen, continued her studies at the school, Marie, at seventeen, had completed hers and was home, assisting her mother in the lace business.

The business itself was run by Louis in an office on the street floor of the house, separate from the family quarters on the floor above. There, in the narrow rooms of their quarters, amid the overstuffed Victorian furniture, the Martins conducted their lives, separated by preference from the world outside the door.

The day began for the family with five-thirty Mass at Notre Dame Church, up the street from the house, attended by the parents and the older girls. The youngest was left at home with the maid. The Martins were esteemed by the priests of Notre Dame. In an era that restricted the reception of the Eucharist, Louis and Zélie were permitted the host three or four times a week, an unusual dispensation. When financial aid was sought for the poor of the parish, the Martins were solicited for it. Louis was known in the town as an easy mark for beggars, giving out money whether approached for it or not. Zélie appears to have kept informed of the needy families in the parish. "How many times," the maid, Louise Marais, was to testify, "was I in the homes of the poor with a hot meal, bottles of wine and coins worth forty sous, and nobody knew of it but us two."

Zélie's letters, perhaps from humility, do not refer to her works of charity. She also doesn't mention any social exchange, a cup of tea, a friendly visit, with her neighbors. Louis was active in the men's Catholic Club at church, but we don't hear of him bringing home any of the men after a meeting for a companionable glass of wine. Marie and Pauline kept in touch with their boarding-school friends by letter but not with visits. If there were guests for Sunday dinner, they were limited to priests from the parish.

31

The Martins as a family were intensely private, devoted to their own interests, an entity unto themselves. Ties were maintained with Zélie's sister, Dosithée, and with their brother, Isidore Guérin, the pharmacist in Lisieux, and his family. Business dealings were a necessary interruption in the family's privacy, but the door was otherwise kept shut on outside intrusions, for a single-minded purpose.

Life, in the view of the parents, indoctrinated in the daughters, was essentially a preparation for the afterlife to come. Heaven, or the homeland, as Zélie called it, must be earned by strict observance of God's laws, as manifested by Christ's ministry on earth. The church of Rome was to be obeyed in its decrees, as well as the pope, the vicar of Christ on earth, in his pronouncements. The goal of heaven must never be far from one's thoughts, and the world, with its vanities, distractions, temptations, not be allowed to tamper with the daily practice of one's religious obligations, for that was what life was all about, a preparation for heaven, nothing more nor less.

Such a regime, of whatever persuasion, imposed by the parents on the children, often has provoked rebellion, the overthrow of authority by the grown children. To the contrary, the Martins' daughters seem to have readily adopted their parents' convictions for their own, including the idea that the highest expression of one's religious beliefs was to be found, for the daughters, in a nun's vocation, which each was to pursue as her life's objective.

Zélie, as late as 1877, still sighed over her rejection by the Sisters of Charity. "I am thinking of the cloister," she writes wistfully in a letter that year to Pauline at boarding school. "I really do not understand, with my inclinations, that it was not my vocation to enter a convent…I should like to grow very old, to withdraw into solitude, once my children are taken care of."

Life for Zélie was not to be long, and her desire for the cloister remained unfulfilled, except through her daughters. Rather than waste her energies on regrets, she applied herself vigorously to her role of wife, mother and business woman, careful to give full value to each, at the ruin of her health, yet sadly always to regard hers as the lesser vocation.

Let us take a closer, more intimate look at the family that occupies the narrow rooms of the house at 36 Rue St. Blaise in Alençon—today a shrine—to learn what we can of their lives. Of narrow focus or not, depending on one's perspective, we observe no shortage of laughter and joy among them, nor of the mutual love and respect that bind them together in their common cause of earning heaven by their daily efforts. But also we can in some instances glimpse the seeds of future heartbreak for them and the basis for the emotional storms to come.

The family's structure is clearly defined. While Louis Martin is accorded deference as the head of the family, it is Zélie who is its heart and soul, the driving force that unites it. She is everywhere in the lives of her girls, arbiter, confidant, dispenser of advice and concern. Louis, by contrast, is a quiet, gentle presence, seeming to hover on the periphery of the family circle, looking on as through a window. Louis's interests, apart from his wife and daughters, and the lace business, are solitary. He enjoys the sport of fishing, casting his rod in the nearby river Sarthe and bringing his catch home for supper. He has purchased a small property, with a pavilion and garden, in the countryside south of the town. There he goes, alone, still with dreams of the great monastery moored in the snows of the Swiss Alps, to meditate in the peace and quiet of nature. Louis's quest for solitude, unlike his wife's, implies a certain estrangement from life and is perhaps symptomatic of the illness that will strike him later.

Now to the Martins' five daughters. Marie, the eldest, old-maidish at seventeen, is rock solid and dependable. She assists her mother in the lace cooperative, supervises the household, and is charged with instructing her two youngest sisters in reading and writing to prepare them for school. Pauline, at sixteen, is finishing her studies at the boarding school in Le Mans but is home for the holidays and summer vacations. Self-assured and mature for her age, and her mother's confidant, Pauline, by reason of her commanding personality, is the most influential of the sisters with the parents, listened to, adhered to, though not always alert to the sensitivities of those around her.

If there is a problem daughter in the family, it is Léonie, the third eldest and the least gifted. Clumsy and inarticulate, possibly mentally disabled, hampered by her deep sense of inferiority, but loving and tender-hearted, Léonie struggles to secure a place for herself in the hierarchy.

Céline, eight years old, is the prettiest of the sisters, piquant, delicate of feature, a dark-eyed beauty, as her photographs testify. Impetuous, she does not hesitate to assert her rights and privileges, but as often as not, having scored a victory, Céline will surrender it to another's strident claim.

And that individual, of course, is the youngest of the Martins, the baby, the family darling, doubly precious for her life having been spared in infancy. Already, at four, she is a force to be reckoned with, not to be overlooked, if she can help it. Indeed, she is the ascending star of the family, the converging center of attention for all of them, by turn adorable minx and wailing penitent, defiant and meek, proud and humble, in quicksilver shifts of her character.

She is both the mistress and the victim of an extreme sensitivity, antennae able to pick up the slightest tremor in the air, susceptible to the least stimulus. She is, moreover, possessed of an intelligence preternatural to her age and of an unerring perception of things as they are, qualities that in equal measure predict for her a glorious or an ignominious future.

Thérèse writes of her earliest years, "God was pleased to surround me with love, and the first memories I have are stamped with smiles and caresses."

Let us listen, not only to her account, but to what was said about her in the family's letters of those years, with affection and much insight into her character.

Here, in a letter of Zélie's to Pauline at boarding school, in 1876, is a delightful sketch of Thérèse at two and a half years: "It's difficult to see how the little monkey got her sweet temper; so obstinate that you can't do anything with her. Once she has said, 'No,' nothing will make her budge. One could put her in the cellar all day, and she'd sleep there rather than say, 'Yes.'"

Again, in another letter months later to Pauline, Zélie writes, 'Little Thérèse asked me the other day if she would go to Heaven. I told her, yes, if she was good. She answered, 'If I'm not good, I'll go to hell, but I know what I will do about it. I will fly to you in Heaven, and what will God be able to do to take me away? You will be holding me tightly in your arms.' I could see in her eyes she was really convinced that God could do nothing to her if she were in her mother's arms."

And, in Zélie's letter to Pauline still later, "As soon as she does anything wrong, everybody must know of it. Yesterday she tore off a small piece of wallpaper. She wanted to tell her father of it immediately. You would have pitied her to see her anxiety. When he returned hours later, and everybody had forgotten about it, she ran at once to Marie, saying, 'Hurry, tell Papa I tore the paper.' Then she awaited her punishment like a criminal. The idea in her little head is that, if she owns up to something, she will be forgiven more easily."

These excerpts from Zélie's letters show us a child of irrepressible spirit and ingenuousness, capable of thinking for herself, in startling turns of her mind, independent of what she has been taught to believe. In another letter to Pauline, Zélie comments, "It's true, she has very rare answers for one her age. Céline said the other day, 'How is it that God can be present in a little Host?' The little one said, 'That is not surprising. God is all-powerful.' 'What does that mean?' 'It means He can do what he wants.'"

It is regrettable that some of her hagiographers will not permit Thérèse to be the child she was. The halo must always be perched on her head. No thought or action must be less than edifying. For example, in her memories of the early years, Thérèse describes her howls of protest at being left home with the maid while the family went to morning Mass. That would be a child's natural reaction to exclusion from her family's activities, but it doesn't satisfy some of her admirers. A popular anecdote in books has her running from the maid, out into the pouring rain, sobbing and distraught, and up the street to the church, as though her motive was to obtain the sanctifying grace of the Mass. No documentation exists of the incident, but it is nevertheless attributed to her.

One famous story of a choice she *did* make as a child is authentic, for she tells it herself in her memories. "One day, Léonie, thinking she was too big to be playing with dolls," the story goes, "came to us [Céline and Thérèse] with a basket of dresses and materials for making dresses, her doll resting on top, and said, 'Here, my little ones, *choose,* I'm giving all this to you.' Céline stretched out her hand and took a little ball of wool. After a moment's reflection, I stretched out mine and said, 'I choose all,' and took the whole basket without further ceremony."

Thérèse would not forget later on her choice of the entire basket. She writes that it represented a summary of her life. "Later on, when I understood that to become a saint, one had to suffer much, seek out the most perfect thing to do, and to forget self...I cried out, *my God, I choose all*...I fear only one thing, to keep my own will, so take it, for I choose all that You will for me."

But we are still dealing with a child, Thérèse, lively and inquisitive, aspiring to goodness, responding to love by giving love. She does not require embellishment in the sunshine of happiness that marked the years until she was four, years in which the shadows were not yet apparent to her.

Within the safe, snug harbor of the family circle, protected from the storms of the world outside, the child flourished, with scarcely anything to trouble her other than an overactive imagination fearful of the dark. Céline, four years older, was her erstwhile companion in play and games, not without the usual spats and disputes. Both were intensely competitive, though the older gave in to the younger more often than not. The love between them fostered a touching dependence, each upon the other, so that even the briefest separation was painful to endure. Thérèse would write of it, "I really wasn't able to be without Céline," in a plaintive note of helplessness, a sign again of her extreme sensitivity.

No one in the family was more captivated by the child than her father. Just the sight of her would bring a smile beaming on the face of Louis Martin. He could not do enough to indulge her whims and fancies or spend enough time with her. It is probable that the closest that Louis, shut off, sequestered in himself, was able to relate to with anyone, was with Thérèse.

Pauline, of the four sisters, resourceful, ever the teacher to the eager, compliant pupil, soon become the child's ideal. Thérèse would stand at the window, gazing toward the railroad station for the train that would deliver Pauline home from boarding school to her. Tears were shed at every departure. It followed that Thérèse would want to imitate her ideal. "I'd often heard it said that Pauline would become a religious," she writes. "Without knowing much about it, I thought, 'I too will be a religious.'"

It also follows, given the emphasis the Martins placed on a religious vocation for their daughters, that Thérèse would assume it for herself. As in every family, the relationships she formed as a child, the influences that shaped her, would exert a lifelong influence on her, not always to her benefit, and sometimes to her despair and grief. At age four, those darker components of life were strangers to her, but the time was growing imminent when she would meet them face to face.

How to conclude this picture of her earliest years in a way that best sums up who she was and what she had learned from the lessons taught her? There is no better indication than to quote from the first words ever written by her. These words are contained in a postscript to a letter that Pauline, home for the Easter holidays, was finishing to a friend, Louise Magdaleine, at boarding school. It is evening, and Pauline's pen toils on. The subject of a good part of the letter is perched on her lap, in the soft glow of an oil lamp in the parlor. Having run out of topics, Pauline adds, "Thérèse is sending you a little message," whereupon she guides the quill pen in the chubby hand of her eager pupil.

PART ONE: Death of a Nun, 1897

"I don't know who you are," the postscript reads, *"but I love you very much just the same."*

There is, if we pronounce them slowly, and ponder the meaning, a solemn cadence to the words, as in a march to the muffled beat of a drum. "I...don't know...who you are...but I love you...very much...just the same."

What do the words spell out for us but the future credo of Thérèse, who wrote them? Surely, the presence of her message amounts to a prophecy of her mission to the world, or so one interpretation might claim for her.

It is poignant to note that the letter is dated April 1877, when already the shadows were fast encroaching on the sunshine of the child's happiness.

Zélie was by then dying.

The tumor in her breast, benign for years, had turned malignant, diagnosed as terminal by the doctors. Since no medical or surgical options were available to her, Zélie, ever practical and zealous in her duties, set to the task of putting her house in order. She sold the lace business, for what evidently was a sizable profit. The money, wisely invested by Louis, would make her family financially secure from then on.

As for the children, Zélie was confident that the two eldest, Marie and Pauline, were fully equipped to rear the two youngest, but she worried about her third child. "Ah! When I no longer will be here, who will care for my poor Léonie? Who will love her?" she pleaded with Marie. As her mother wished, Léonie was cared for by her sisters, but her pitiful struggles, her humiliating defeats at finding her own life, would go on haphazardly.

Zélie, in a renewed surge of energy, made a last-ditch fight for her life. In June 1877 she embarked with Marie, Pauline and

Léonie on a desperate journey to Lourdes, a town in the Pyrenees in the south of France. It had been the scene in the 1850s of what were said to be the visions of the Blessed Virgin in a cave to the peasant girl, Bernadette Soubirous. Water had sprung from the rocks in the cave, believed to be of a miraculous nature. A church was built on the site, and Lourdes became a shrine, sanctioned by Rome. Pilgrims from around the world flocked to Lourdes, the sick, the blind, the paralyzed, to bathe in the waters, in the hope, as Zélie hoped, for a cure that medicine could not provide.

The train journey over jolting mountain rails was arduous, the lodgings primitive, the swarming crowds threatening. Although Zélie returned to Alençon without a cure, she was at peace with herself. If the Mother of God had not cured her, she counseled, in the last letter from her hand, it was because "my time is up, and God wills me to repose elsewhere than on this earth."

Stoic as always, Zélie attended to the final disposition of her illness. Thérèse and Céline were sent each day to the house of their cousins, the Leriches, to spare them the sights and cries of their mother's suffering. Deathbed visits, common during the Victorian era, were made by Isidore Guérin and Mme. Guérin, traveling from Lisieux. The last farewell look exchanged with the dying woman would remain fixed in her sister-in-law's memory. "I believe I understood that look, and nothing will ever make me forget it," Mme. Guérin wrote years later to Thérèse. "I tried to take the place of she whom God had taken from you."

At dawn, August 20, 1877, at the age of forty-six, Zélie Martin breathed her last. The next day, after a Requiem Mass at Notre Dame Church, she was buried in the family plot in the cemetery in Alençon, alongside the graves of her four lost children.

And what was the effect of a mother's death on her four-year-old daughter? Thérèse was spared nothing of the paraphernalia of death that enveloped the house on Rue St. Blaise. She was witness to the last rites of the church administered by a priest to her gasping, writhing mother. She happened upon the coffin tilted upright against the wall, waiting to receive the deceased's body. Lifted up to the bedside by her father, she kissed for the last time the cold waxen mask of her mother's face. She stood with the family at the grave, staring at the coffin as it was lowered into the dug-up ground and the earth was shoveled over it.

The next day, the five sisters were seated together in mute commiseration. "Poor little things," Louise, the maid, clucked at Céline and Thérèse. "Poor little mites, you have no mother anymore." A sobbing Céline flung herself into Marie's arms, declaring that she would be her mother, and Thérèse made the same declaration with Pauline, sealing, as it were, their relationship forever.

Irretrievable loss had struck at the family's soul, and recovery from it would be the next step.

In November 1877, two months after their loss, the Martins bid goodbye to Alençon. Isidore Guérin had been searching for a suitable house for them in Lisieux, so that the girls might benefit from the maternal care Aunt Guérin had promised Zélie that she would provide. Uncle Isidore advised Louis by letter of a wonderful house and gardens, on a hilltop above the ancient town, available for rent or sale. Louis, after a trip to inspect the property, signed a long-term lease for it, and there the family moved, for what was, as she would state, the second and saddest period in the life of Thérèse.

However, the deep after-shock of her mother's death was slow to surface in the child. The gift of sensitivity that enabled her, like the boy Mozart or the youth Raphael, to soar in mind and spirit above the skies, above the stars, would, in reversal, render her vulnerable, the victim of the least assault against her.

4.

If we look at this second period of Thérèse's childhood, the six years from age four to ten, what we see is the downward trajectory of a child from the pure light of utter security and trust that shone on her into the nether regions of the darkness below.

She appeared at first to be recovering from her mother's death, regarding the move to Lisieux as an adventure to be enjoyed. The loving home she had known in Alençon was re-created, to the extent that it could be, at Les Buissonnets, the name the family gave to the property in Lisieux. Marie and Pauline efficiently took charge of the household and of the lessons to prepare the two youngest girls for school. Pauline was especially mindful of her role as the mother Thérèse had taken for herself and of her duties as the child's spiritual guide. She was less conscious, it would seem, of the consequences should she not be there for the child to run to with her emotional needs.

As before, Céline and Thérèse were companions in the daily routine prescribed for them, the mornings at play, lessons in the afternoons. Les Buissonnets offered them a wide range of pursuits. The property included gardens, front and back, for tending flowers and vegetables, a hen coop to collect eggs from, and a rabbit hutch with furry, whiskered pets to hug and feed carrots to. The fruit trees in the garden yielded in season tart Norman apples and pears for the plucking. Victoire, the family's maid, cook and laundress, swore that the two were pests, little scamps, always underfoot, but she swore it with undisguised affection for them. It was a treat when Aunt Guérin regularly dropped by the house with her daughters, Jeanne and Marie, playmates for their cousins. Sundays were often spent at the Guérins' home above the pharmacy, where Thérèse was struck timid and dumb in the presence of her somber and magisterial Uncle Isidore.

A belvedere, a kind of enclosed windowed porch, which afforded a sweeping view of the countryside, was built into the roof of the house. Just as Louis Martin had gone to the pavilion in Alençon to sequester himself in solitude, so he sought it in the belvedere. Afternoons, however, the solitude was interrupted by his favorite daughter, come to show him the marks she'd earned for her lessons that day. It was as if she had another purpose in coming. The reclusive Louis discovered in Thérèse someone able to pierce through the barrier of his reserve, who instinctively understood his quest for solitude, as though it were part of herself, too. In the deepening attachment between them, father and daughter would go off on walks of the town, stopping at St. Jacques, the parish church, or at the Cathedral of St. Pierre, where the family worshiped, to light a candle and pray. They ventured one day to the chapel of the Carmelite monastery on the outskirts of Lisieux. The mystery of the nuns hidden behind the choir grille across from her intrigued Thérèse, though she had no idea of the monastery's significance in her future.

Louis, as always, was a friend to the town's destitute, but now his daughter was awarded the privilege of almsgiving. She would remember the crippled old man in ragged clothes, hobbling along on crutches, who in shame and pride had refused her coins. "I cannot express the feeling that went through my heart," she writes of the encounter. "I wanted to console that man, and instead I had caused him pain." And, "I'd heard that on our First Communion

Day, we could obtain whatever we asked for. I'll pray for this man on that day, I vowed, and five years later I kept my promise."

Thérèse liked best the long, observing walks in the countryside with Louis that nurtured her love of nature. The hills and fields, the meandering brooks and streams, flashing silver in the sun, and the wildflowers, the daisies, cornflowers, buttercups and cowslips that in spring embroidered the green hills, to gather and bring home in great bunches, were a wonder to her. How beautiful, the blue, the dome of heaven…was that where her mother had gone to live with God?

She accompanied her father on his fishing expeditions, angling her rod in the rushing river or else content to sit in quiet reflection on the grassy banks. She would remember vividly the night when, bound home with Louis, she'd dawdled behind him for a moment, caught up in the starry radiance of the firmament. Enthralled, she'd pointed a finger at the cluster of stars in the Belt of Orion. "The 'T'…do you see it, Papa?" she'd called to him. "Look, my name is written in heaven."

So life, then, home, the family, was much the same as before, but it was not the same. Change was happening, all through the happy scenes we have described above. Change, and the creeping shadows it brought, had begun within two months of the family's move to Lisieux.

And the change, in each instance, involved a sense of loss in a child already made vulnerable by loss.

January 2, 1878, was the occasion of Thérèse's fifth birthday. A few mornings later, when Céline left her to start classes at the school of the Benedictine Abbey in town, the child felt that she'd lost the person she couldn't really do without. How she must have haunted the garden gate that afternoon, peering desperately down the road for Céline to return to her. While they were reunited each afternoon, still, she felt the loss again in the morning. She had not, in fact, recovered from her mother's death. It had left a wound in her, passed unnoticed by her elders, that had not healed.

There were good times in the midst of the shadows. The summer of 1878 was Thérèse's first visit to the seashore. She went with her father and sisters on a day's outing to Trouville, the resort on the Normandy coast, a short train ride from Lisieux. She sat on a rock, she tells us, staring out at the sea. The blue immensity of the sea was God's immensity, and the glory of a flaming sunset over the sea was God's glory. The Guérins each summer rented a villa in Trouville or the neighboring Deauville, and they invited their nieces for a stay, so Thérèse was to delight in many seashore visits.

In the summer of 1880, a disturbing incident occurred that indicates the precariousness of the child's emotional stability in its continual descent, again occasioned by a fear of loss.

It is August. Thérèse, age seven, is at a window of the belvedere, looking down at the garden. Louis Martin is away on one of his business trips to Alençon. From the window she glimpses in the garden a man she takes to be her father, though he is old and stooped and a shroud-like cloth covers his head, concealing his face from her. As the man shuffles along the garden path, she cries out, *"Papa,"* in fright, *"Papa,"* at which the man, or her ghostly vision of him, vanishes into the air.

The memory of the vision would be fixed indelibly in her mind. It would be years before she felt she understood the import of its tragic message concerning her father. But for the child at the window the message was of loss, the fear of a cycle of loss, sprung from her mother's death.

Thérèse had yet to step beyond the shelter of the family circle. Her contacts with the world outside were all but non-existent.

Then in October, 1881, a few months short of her eighth birthday, she was enrolled at the school of the Benedictine Abbey, where Céline was a student. Thanks to the lessons at home, she was placed above her age level in a class of older girls, to distressing results. Every classroom has its bullies of either sex, who prey on the vulnerable among them. Thérèse was not exempt from the taunts and jeers of her classmates. Unable to defend herself, rebuffed by the girls, she withdrew from them, a loner, wandering the schoolyard at recreation, looking on at the roughhouse games of play. Unable to join in, she occupied herself with collecting the dead birds from under the trees for Christian burial. A morbid inclination, surely, but one that reflects the sadness in her, worsening day by day.

At home she spoke only of her schoolwork, the scholarship that would win her medals and ribbons of achievement. At school each day she endured the taunts and derision of the girls in silence. Céline, in an upper grade, with a different schedule, could give her no support. Indeed, Céline and the family were not aware of the troubles Thérèse was having. She had steeled herself never to complain, never to defend herself. She opted for silence, by an act of will that later in Carmel would rise to heroism, and perhaps was approximated in the child of eight.

Here we touch upon the contradiction in this very strange child—extreme vulnerability paired with an inner core of strength that was her armor against attack. Nor was she the only source of the strength within her fragile self. Thérèse has told us who from the beginning was her teacher, and that, despite her emotional upheaval, this spared her from ultimate harm. She would give us a luminous example of her blessed teacher's guidance, as she interpreted it for herself, but that was two years away from her present woes.

Meanwhile, she reported dutifully to the Abbey that spring, shunned by her classmates and praised by the teachers for her scholarship, which doubtless contributed to the jeers and taunts. More and more, as the summer with its brief reprieve at the seashore went by, she relied on Pauline for sustenance. Pauline was the security blanket she clung to, seeking her out for the little conferences between them, the reassuring talk of God and eternity.

If the fear of loss hounded the child, she was about to be pitched by the shock of it, beyond reach, into the darkness.

October 2, 1882: Pauline is gone from Les Buissonnets.

That morning, while Céline and Thérèse went off to the Abbey, Pauline traveled across town with her father, Marie and Léonie to the Carmelite monastery, and through the gates to the chapel. Goodbyes, embraces were exchanged, after which Pauline went down the hall to the door of the cloister, barred to outsiders. She then stepped through the door, to the nuns within the enclosure. As the door swung shut behind her, she had, to use the phrase common at the time, left the world. Henceforth, she was no longer Pauline Martin, but Sister Agnes of Jesus, postulant in the Order of Discalced Carmelite nuns, which traced its origins over the centuries to the ancient Mount of Carmel in the desert of Palestine, where the first Christian hermits had lived in solitude, to worship God in silence, work and mortification.

Thérèse was familiar with the Order's history. She tells us of a game she played as a child in the garden with her cousin, Marie Guérin, pretending to be hermits in the desert, erecting altars in niches in the garden wall. She records a conversation she had with Pauline, of childish but serious intent. "I said to Pauline that I would like to be a hermit, and go away with her to a far-off desert place. She answered that my desire was also hers, and that she was waiting for me to be big enough for her to leave." Hatched in the child's mind was the idea that when Pauline left home to pursue her desire, she would, of course, go with her.

But now, to her shocked dismay, Pauline had betrayed her trust and left without her. In a family that prized a religious vocation above any other, the shock wasn't that Pauline had entered Carmel. It was that she had not waited until Thérèse could accompany her. To compound the shock, Pauline's departure had been kept secret from her. She'd learned of it by chance, when she'd overheard Pauline discussing her plans with Marie.

Her adopted mother was gone, and where she'd gone was beyond the child's reach. She could not wait for her to return at the garden gate, as she'd waited for Céline. She felt in her numbing shock as if for the second time she had lost her mother.

The family was permitted a weekly visit with Pauline in the speak room of the monastery, exempt from the rule of silence. The Martins, and often the Gúerins, would assemble at one side of the room. Across the room, behind the grille that separated her from the others, would be seated Sister Agnes. The visit was strictly limited to half an hour. In her effort to portion the minutes among each of the family, Agnes didn't quite get around to the youngest member. She was ignored, passed over, the minutes ticking away to the visit's end, tears glistening in her eyes, but without a word of protest from her lips. Would the next visit be different? No, it would not, she would learn to her despair.

Life went on for Thérèse, or rather, a life in which the hour was fixed perpetually at twilight. She went to the Abbey, always the loner, faithful to her lessons. At home, she appeared to her family to be the same obedient, endearing child, never complaining, quieter, perhaps, more introspective. As the season changed from winter to spring to summer, she developed chronic headaches, the classic symptom of a worsening neurosis, but the family attributed it to the strain of her schoolwork. In fact, her nervous system was strained to the breaking point. It wasn't until March 1883 that it broke, and the process of disorientation capitulated the ten year old into the darkness, beyond the help of her family, too late to remedy it.

March 28, Easter Sunday, 1883: Louis Martin, for whom travel is one of the few pleasures he allows himself, is in Paris for the holidays with Mariet and Léonie. Céline and Thérèse are staying with Aunt and Uncle Guérin, in their home above the pharmacy. The day that began with the joyous celebration of Easter Mass at St. Pierre is not to conclude in joy. Toward evening, the twilight in which Thérèse has existed, consumes her. She is seized by a violent trembling of her body. Aunt Guérin puts her to bed, wrapped in blankets, warmed by a hot-water bottle. Her niece, she decides, is coming down with one of her colds.

But that diagnosis is mistaken. All that night and into morning, the seizures grow uncontrollable. The child is hallucinating, babbling incoherently, her bulging eyes wild and catatonic, as if her sanity is at risk. Uncle Guérin, alarmed, consults with Dr. Notta, the family's physician, whose opinion is that the child is suffering from a nervous disorder, surely not fatal, but he prescribes no medication. By nightfall of Monday, with no improvement in the patient's condition, and death perhaps hovering over the bed, Uncle Guérin sends a telegram to Paris, which brings Louis and his daughters hastening to Lisieux by the next train, stunned at the demented, babbling creature staring up at them from the bed.

So critical is the child's condition, the seizures that attack her body, the hysteria, the hallucinations, that for two days she cannot be moved home from the Guérins. When she is back in her own room again, it is hoped that Les Buissonnets, the familiar surroundings, the scenes of happy memories, will aid in her recovery, but that is not to transpire.

She cannot for a moment be left unattended. Marie is her nurse, day and night at the bedside, the lost "Mama" to whom she clings. The symptoms have multiplied, fits of agitation that alternate with a deathlike coma. She must on occasion be tied by rope to the bed to prevent her from flinging herself howling to the floor. Strange monsters materialize before her terrified gaze. Since she dare not be left alone, when Marie exits the room, Victoire, the maid, assumes the vigil, and then the child cries out in nameless fright, screaming, shrieking until Marie reappears.

It is to be expected, in a family for whom religion is the prime consideration, above medical science, that prayers are being offered for the child's recovery. A storm of prayers, joined with those of Agnes and the Carmelites, besieges the heavens. Louis Martin has sent money to the Church of Our Lady of Victories in Paris for a novena of Masses in the child's behalf. A statue of the Virgin Mary, as Our Lady of Victories, a popular devotion of the time, stands guard on a table by the sickbed. The statue had been Zélie's, constantly prayed to by her, and is revered by the family as a holy relic.

But the prayers do not ask simply for a recovery. No, the petitioning is for nothing less than a miraculous cure.

And that, Thérèse tells us, is exactly what was granted to her.

Just as the illness had begun on Sunday, the cure, as she regarded it, occurred as suddenly, two dragging months later, on a

Sunday in May, held by long Christian tradition to be Mary's month.

It is afternoon. The patient's condition in the sickroom at Les Buissonnets remains the same as yesterday and the preceding weeks. The exhausted child lies in her bed, supine for the moment. Marie is downstairs in the garden, enjoying a respite from her nursing duties. Léonie has relieved her in the sickroom and is reading a book at the window. The child stirs fretfully in her bed and calls in a low moan for Marie. The moaning escalates into a piercing scream, audible in the garden below, that brings Marie hurrying up the stairs. The child appears to be in the grip of some unknown terror devouring her. Marie leans over the bed, and the child stares wildly at her without recognition, possessed by some monstrous, terrifying apparition. It seems to Marie that the crisis of the illness is at hand—will death be the outcome? Unable to provide any assistance, frantic, Marie and Léonie turn, as no doubt they have done before, to the statue on the table by the bed. The sisters fall to their knees, beseeching the Virgin to intercede for the afflicted child, who, too, has pinned her frightened gaze upon the statue in a wordless plea for help.

What happened next, as Thérèse reports it, was that, as suddenly as the illness, the dementia, had incapacitated her, it was lifted from her. She was cured, all in an instant, and she knew beyond questioning the source of her cure.

The child, a moment ago raving and demented, sits up in her bed with shining eyes. She calls to her kneeling sisters. "The Virgin smiled at me...ah, never was a smile as beautiful as hers...it...it's a miracle," she cried.

PART TWO

The Master's Hand
1897

I always find a way to be happy.

5.

Death had come for Sister Thérèse at seven-thirty in the evening of September 30, 1897. The timing was inconvenient, in that it threw off the daily schedule of the nuns. Having spent the entire day at the bedside, by order of the prioress, Mother de Gonzague, while the death agony dragged on, the nuns had dispersed to their various duties of work and prayer. Supper, usually held at five o'clock, had been moved to a later hour.

Thérèse still lay in the bed in the infirmary where she had breathed her last choking gasp of breath. A small, low-ceilinged, claustrophobic room on the ground floor of the monastery, stifling in the summer heat just passed, acutely depressing, the infirmary's one virtue was the two large windows that overlooked the cloister garden and the meadow beyond. It was a view that earlier Thérèse, sick and confined to her bed, had often turned to for consolation. Sometimes, on lovely summer days, she would be wheeled out on a portable reclining chair to the cloister walk, to be among her beloved flowers and greenery. Such intervals, interrupted by a coughing fit or hemorrhage, were brief, and back into the infirmary she was wheeled. Well, it wasn't as if her approaching death was unexpected. She had felt from an early age—not a presentiment, really—that hers was not to be a long life, and so it had proven to be.

All that remained were the final disposing acts of her funeral and burial.

Gathered at the bed, to prepare her for burial, were her three sisters, Mother Agnes of Jesus; Sister Marie of the Sacred Heart, who had been Marie Martin, eldest of the sisters; and by no means last, Sister Géneviéve, the ubiquitous Céline Martin, seldom without an opinion on almost anything and ever ready to make it known. All three had wanted a closer relationship with Thérèse in the Carmel. "We are not at home, under the parental roof," she would explain about the distance she kept from their company. The Rule does not allow for family ties, she would say, which more or less fell on deaf ears.

For Agnes, especially, to get through the next few days and to attend to her duties were her only goals. The cause she so ardently believed in must wait, as the manuscripts must wait, until she was better able to deal with such matters. The obituary? No, she could not deal with it, either, to say nothing of the task at hand.

Still, it must be done, and with her sisters Agnes set to the task.

The emaciated body was stripped of its frilly nightcap and gown. The body was washed, cleansed of any vestige of the disease that might cling to it. The cropped, matted, perspiration-soaked hair was washed, rinsed, and swept back from the brow. Somehow, the washing, rather than worsening their grief, rallied the sisters. It reaffirmed the cause they believed in, for they were preparing a saint for her last viewing by mortal eyes.

The body of Thérèse was dressed in the ill-fitting Carmelite habit she had worn in life. A coffin stood ready in the next room, and nuns were arriving to offer assistance. The body was laid out in the plain, narrow pine box. A crown of white roses, symbol of the martyrdom of a nun's life, was placed on the black-veiled head, and flowers were strewn about her in the coffin.

There would be, appropriately, no shortage, indeed, a profusion of flowers at the ceremonies. Some were plucked from the convent garden, others, splendid sprays and wreaths of lilies, roses, carnations, chrysanthemums, were sent by family members and friends of the family. The image of a flower, "a little white flower," as she described it, was one that Thérèse had chosen for herself.

The coffin, thus adorned, was carried in procession through the bare rabbits' warren of halls in the monastery to the chapel, where it was installed in the nuns' choir directly below the altar, and there it would repose for a wake of two nights, after which a Requiem Mass would be offered for the soul of the deceased.

For two nights, then, the open coffin stood in the choir of the chapel. Each night, family members, priests associated with the Carmel, and its friends and benefactors assembled in the visitors' gallery to pray for and trade reminiscences of the nun in the coffin. The family was represented by Léonie Martin, the fifth of the sisters, beloved of Thérèse; Uncle and Aunt Guérin, intimately involved in her earlier years at home; their daughter, Jeanne, and her husband, Dr. Francis La Néele, who had, a month before, been summoned by the prioress to examine the dying patient, and was the last of the family outside the cloister to have seen her alive. The Guérins' younger daughter, Marie, now Sister Marie of the Eucharist, of the band of believers, was seated with the nuns in the choir.

All of the family members were numb with grief at the loss of she who had been precious to them onward from her birth. Their grief, too, was for Louis Martin, father of the five daughters, the shy and reclusive Louis, who had died in 1894. Perhaps it was just as well, it was agreed, that Louis had not lived to experience the suffering and death of his "queen."

The wake of two nights, followed by the Mass and burial, was a ritual accorded to each nun in the Carmel who had died, but in some particulars this one was unlike any that had preceded it.

There was the startling vision of Thérèse in her flower-strewn coffin, a crucifix clasped in her hands. Her face, upraised on a pillow and turned slightly to the side, betrayed none of the ravages of the disease that had killed her. Instead, her face in death gave forth a serene and undefiled beauty, the lips parted slightly in a smile. It was the subject of much commentary by those who had viewed the coffin. The whisperings of the nuns spoke as well of the fragrance of roses, which seemed to permeate not only the chapel and the halls beyond, but the entire monastery.

On the morning of October 4, 1897, the Requiem Mass was said in the chapel for the repose of the soul of Sister Thérèse. The coffin was nailed shut, and since the convent cemetery was full, it was transported by horse and funeral carriage, followed by a carriage of mourners, to the town cemetery of Lisieux. The final burial rites were performed at the grave site, and the coffin was lowered into the earth. A simple wooden cross and nameplate marked the grave of Thérèse in the rows of graves. By December, it would be twice buried in the snows of the harsh Norman winter storms. For months the grave would be as hidden as her life had been.

So it appeared that the end had come for Thérèse in the bare, lonely ground of the town cemetery.

But as events would swiftly indicate, it was not the end but only the beginning.

Exactly when, in the days immediately after the burial, Mother Agnes got the idea of how the manuscripts might be published, despite the obstacles looming against publication, is not recorded for us.

She would have preferred to retreat into seclusion with her grief, but that wasn't feasible. Not only was the obituary, still to be written and sent out, pressing at her for attention, but there was another charge she could not ignore. Thérèse had entrusted the publication of the manuscripts to her alone, although her surviving siblings, Sister Marie and Sister Génevéve as well as Mother Agnes, together with Léonie Martin, were the legal heirs of the manuscripts.

"It could be an important work of God's, and it mustn't be hindered," Thérèse had said to Agnes, before her death. "You mustn't speak to anyone about it before the publication. You must speak only to Mother Prioress."

Agnes was all too aware that the existing manuscripts were not ready for publication. Extensive editing, corrections, adjustments and transpositions of certain passages needed to be done. Nor was there sufficient text, as it existed, to make a book of any length. Selections from the author's letters, the last conversations of the dying patient, preserved in notebooks, would have to be added to round out the text. That, for Agnes, would be a sacred responsibility to carry out, but it would not eliminate the other obstacles that faced her. The prioress must approve of the publication, and it would require the seal of *Nihil Obstat* to signify that the text contained nothing objectionable or contrary to church teaching.

Agnes's concerns were perhaps a case of putting the cart before the horse. Competing for her attention was the obituary, still not composed or sent out. She ought, perhaps, to occupy herself in that regard and not confine her efforts to the manuscripts.

Yes, but what if…what if the two objectives could be combined into one? The more she thought of it, the more the idea took hold of her. Why not publish the manuscripts *as* the obituary, to be sent out accordingly?

"You must speak only to Mother Prioress."

Mindful of that directive, Mother Agnes promptly requested an interview with Mother de Gonzague, the prioress. It was a difficult step to take, given the complicated relations between them, once mutual trust and affection, now deteriorated into mutual antagonism, largely due to the tug of war both had waged over the handling of Thérèse, almost from the day she'd entered the Carmel.

To understand the interaction of these two formidable women, and the consequences of their association, it is necessary to go back a few years, to 1893, and the election of a prioress, crucial to our story...

6.

The prioress of a Carmelite monastery was absolute in her authority over the nuns of her community. Her voice, it was believed by them, was the voice of Christ and was therefore to be obeyed without question, whatever might be thought of her pronouncements. She was elected to office for a term of three years by secret ballot of the nuns. No limit was fixed on the terms she might serve in office, but should the nuns grow dissatisfied with her performance, she could be unseated in the next election.

For twenty-one years, except for one term out of office, the imperious, autocratic, by turn beguiling charmer and unmitigated tyrant, Mother Marie de Gonzague, had held the reins of power at the Lisieux Carmel. We might compare her to a lovable rogue of a U.S. Senator, who, despite his offenses, is continuously returned to office by voters smitten with his charisma.

That, however, for Mother de Gonzague, was about to change.

As the chill light of dawn spread over the Norman sky, the nuns one by one cast their secret ballots. The ballots were counted, and by a narrow margin a new prioress was voted into office. She was, of course, Sister Agnes of Jesus. In her earlier years as a nun, while conscious of Mother de Gonzague's faults, Agnes had vouched fidelity to and shown love and admiration for the woman she would later unseat. A rivalry had sprung up between them. In what was likely a division of the community, the younger nuns versus the older, Agnes had been elected prioress.

She was to occupy the chair of office for only one term. Agnes would, ironically, be unseated by the very woman she had deposed. But during her three years in office Agnes issued an order, a command, that at the time she didn't invest with much seriousness, but which was to exert a profound and lasting impact on the Carmel.

It happened by chance one December night in 1894, while the nuns were gathered in the common for recreation. The austere Carmelite day began in darkness, when a clapper in the halls aroused the nuns from sleep. The day was portioned into equal periods of work and prayer. Supper, the second meal of the day, was at five in the afternoon. It was followed by recreation at six. The rule of all-prevailing silence was suspended for the hour, and the nuns were permitted to converse and amuse themselves with games and songs and the like. In winter, the added attraction of the hour was the warmth of a fire in the chapter room. It was, incredibly, the only source of heat in the frigid cold of the monastery.

Among those gathered by the fire that December night were the Martin sisters, Agnes, Thérèse, Marie, and a fourth, Céline, who by 1894, had joined them in the cloister as Sister Généviéve. Recreation was of special enjoyment for the four sisters. It was the one hour of the day that brought them all together. This distressed Agnes, who was offended by the distance Thérèse otherwise maintained from them.

Mother de Gonzague, dethroned by Agnes, would have been present that night, in her own circle of nuns, at a remove from the sisters. Although she and Agnes displayed a surface politeness in their dealings, rancor was not far below the surface. It dated back to the early days of Thérèse in the Carmel. Agnes was then of the opinion, which she did not hesitate to express, that Mother de Gonzague's treatment of Thérèse was altogether too harsh and restrictive. She chafed at the prioress's repeated criticism of Thérèse's ineptness in the housework assigned to her. "Of course, you would like to see Sister Thérèse given preference," was Mother de Gonzague's tart reply to Agnes's protests, "but I consider precisely the opposite course necessary. Her pride is much greater than others think. She has need of constant humiliation." It was an estimate Thérèse would not have protested, had she known of it, and the unsparing criticism of her went on while Mother de Gonzague was in office.

Later on the nuns said that Thérèse was Mother de Gonzague's spoiled pet. Perhaps, like most of us, they couldn't see the noses plain on their faces.

As prioress, Agnes was now in a position to alleviate the hard, uncompromising path Thérèse was traveling alone, but that was easier said than done. Agnes's real intention was to remain the guiding light she had always been in the life and spiritual quest of her foster child. By then, however, Thérèse had advanced far along the hidden path she had chosen to trod, quite separate and apart from that of her former mentor.

That Thérèse was fully conscious of the offense to Agnes was shown by her conduct at recreation. She sought to compensate for the distance she kept from her sisters by entertaining them with stories of her childhood at home with them. She made it appear as if no change had occurred in their relations in the Carmel.

Thérèse was a superb storyteller, imaginative, dramatic, delightfully humorous, self-deprecating, and her stories, night after night, held her sisters in thrall, always desiring to hear still more.

But then, on that night in December, at recreation, Sister Marie ventured to make a suggestion. What a pity, she remarked, that the stories were not written down, to be kept as a cherished family souvenir.

"*Yes!*" the others chorused enthusiastically, whereupon Agnes, as prioress, commanded that the stories be committed to pen and paper.

Thérèse was flabbergasted by what she heard. She had no ambitions of authorship, and she worried that to focus on herself would distract her from her religious obligations. Still, Agnes as prioress spoke with the voice of Christ and must be obeyed.

A year went by while Thérèse, laboring at odd hours, mostly late at night in her cell, in the dim flicker of an oil lamp, a writing board clamped on her knees, composed in a schoolgirl copybook, to the scratch-scratch of a quill pen, a memoir of her childhood. When the work was finished, she submitted the copybook, silently, on her knees one night in the chapel, to her superior. Agnes, taken up with the duties of her office, had entirely forgotten her command of a year before. Months elapsed before she turned her attention to the memoir. She was struck as if by lightning at the hidden life that, revealed, glowed like a jewel and made of Agnes in an instant the postulator of a cause.

The memoir, Agnes fretted to herself, was incomplete. It told of Thérèse's childhood and growing up, but her life as a Carmelite nun was barely sketched in. The spiritual journey she had made: of what benefit it would be to readers searching for a path to follow! Already the idea of publication had crept into Agnes's mind, nudging at her, and would not go away.

Meanwhile, as the rigors of winter give way to spring, events were conspiring against Agnes's plans. In April of 1896, during

Lent, in the hours between Holy Thursday and Good Friday, Thérèse was shaken awake in her cell by a gush of blood from her lungs rushing into her mouth, staining her nightdress crimson. It seemed in the morning to be a momentary lapse in her robust health. The bloom of youth glowed on her cheeks. A month earlier, in a bitterly contested election for prioress, Agnes had been voted from office, replaced by Mother de Gonzague. Thérèse reported the incident of the blood to the restored prioress. She asked for and was given permission to go on with her duties. No announcement of the hemorrhage was made to the community, nor did Thérèse confide in Agnes or her other sisters of it. A fatal disease had infiltrated her body, waiting merely to manifest itself in full.

In September of that year, as if by some plan not of Agnes's devising, Thérèse was asked by her sister Marie to write of the spiritual revelations she had been granted. By then a pallor rather than a bloom was upon her face, she'd lost weight, her strength was failing her by the day. Nevertheless, in answer to Marie's request, she composed, within a few days, on sheets of notepaper, an account of her spiritual quest of Jesus and the means by which she had achieved it.

Agnes rejoiced at this splendid addition to the memoir. Yet, confronting her, in the months that followed, was the slow-dawning shock of the unthinkable, that her youngest sister was fatally stricken and had not long to live.

By June of 1897, feverish, exhausted by fits of coughing blood, unable to rise from her pallet, Thérèse, relieved of her duties, was confined to her cell. Medical science in the 1890s offered no deterrent to the onslaught of tuberculosis. The presumed remedies—the bloodletting, the cauterizing of the blood by red-hot needles applied to the flesh, such as Dr. Cornière, the monastery's on-call physician, performed on Thérèse—were ineffective. The disease would progress unchecked to her death.

Agnes's shock and distress were accompanied by the fear that the memoir, still unfinished, would never see publication. The testament of a saint to the world would be lost irretrievably. Agnes felt compelled to do all she could to stave off that eventuality. "The poor must always work," Thérèse had said, of her vow of poverty. She would want to be occupied with work of some kind, ill or not, dying or not, of that Agnes was certain.

Ah, but what could she, no longer the prioress, no longer able to issue commands, do to bring it about? Worse, her old adversary was again in office. Mother de Gonzague was unlikely to be sympathetic to any request from one who had often criticized her actions.

Well, if it was pride that Agnes must swallow, undeterred, she swallowed it. Sometime early in June 1897 she went to consult with the prioress. She gave her the memoir, of which the prioress knew nothing, and urged her to read it, worthy, she attested, of publication.

Agnes could not have expected a favorable response from Mother de Gonzague, but that is what she received. Impressed by what she had read, the prioress ordered Thérèse to continue with her writing, as best as she could manage it.

Weeks later, in need of round-the-clock care, Thérèse was carried from her cell down to the infirmary, to what would be her deathbed. There, nursed by her three sisters, she composed her thoughts and observations each day in a school copybook, like the one she had written at Agnes's command. The voice of Christ had spoken and must be obeyed. Despite the ravages of the disease consuming her, she went on with her work, a summation of her beliefs, a last will and testament, as it were. In the final days of her efforts, unable to wield her pen, she wrote in a faltering pencil. The last sentence trailed off the paper, never to be finished, and the pencil fell from her hand.

Two months later, death, "the Thief," as she called it, came for her.

And once again, days after the burial, Agnes went to confer with the prioress. The issue of a proper obituary for Thérèse had not been resolved. Why not, boldly suggested Agnes, publish the memoir and send it to the Carmels as the obituary?

And to that, the prioress agreed, though with a proviso.

The memoir, in the strictest sense, was not what the term implied. Thérèse had left three manuscripts, written at different intervals, from different perspectives, on varying themes. Each was in the form of a letter, since she, a prolific letter writer, was most at ease in that form. The first manuscript, inscribed in the copybook, was addressed to Agnes, and the second, on sheets of notepaper, to Marie. The third manuscript, again in a copybook, was addressed to Mother de Gonzague, and that is what the proviso concerned.

The prioress demanded of Agnes that the manuscripts be altered to make it appear that all three were addressed to her alone, or she would refuse her permission for publication. Rather than risk a refusal, Agnes consented to the demand.

It speaks volumes about Mother de Gonzague's character that she should have made such an outrageous demand. Yet to cast her as the villain in the story, Snow White's evil stepmother, as some biographers have done, would be a serious miscalculation. For all of her flaws, her erratic behavior, her susceptibility to flattery and use of subterfuge, and her unyielding grip on the power of her office,

Mother de Gonzague was blessed with a deep insight into the character and formation of Thérèse. She was not mistaken in her disciplines to rid the young novice of her pride. Thérèse herself tells us of her furious battles to subdue her will, her ego, her pride. "A soul of such mettle must not be treated as a child," the prioress had declared. "Dispensations are not made for her sort. Let her be; *God* supports her."

Mother de Gonzague was no less acute in recognizing the spiritual growth in Thérèse. She had delegated her above others to instruct the novices in their formation. "If I were to appoint a prioress," Mother de Gonzague remarked to a priest visiting the Carmel, "I would select Sister Thérèse out of the whole community. She is perfect in everything. The only fault she has are her three sisters."

Thérèse would not align herself with either faction. Caught in the crossfire between the two adversaries, often its victim, she kept apart from it, and loved both factions unconditionally, without stint. And by so doing, Thérèse affected her superior profoundly.

Mother de Gonzague died in 1904, seven years after her famous daughter. "No person in this house had been as culpable as I," she confessed, as she lay dying of cancer. "Nevertheless, I trust in God and in my little Thérèse. She will win my salvation."

Whatever her demands, by giving Agnes permission to publish the manuscripts, Mother de Gonzague, so baffling and contradictory, helped to give to the world a saint.

Thus did Agnus, the manuscripts spread on the desk before her, begin the process of editing the divergent material into shape. More than likely, she began her work where Thérèse had begun it, with a copybook of her memories of childhood.

"The Springtime Story of a Little White Flower" was the preface appended to the text. How must Agnes have marveled, as she turned the pages of the copybook, correcting the errors in spelling and grammar, at the other evidence that leapt at her from the pages.

It was evidence, above all else, that from the cradle on, in every instance, a Master Hand was at the till, guiding the fragile bark of the child into the turbulent waters of life...

PART THREE

Child of Light
1884

I accept everything out of love of
God, even all sorts of extraordinary
thoughts that come into my mind.

7.

There is preserved in the archives of the Lisieux Carmel a souvenir album, resplendently bound in blue velvet. It is the handiwork of Agnes, a gift to Thérèse to help prepare her for her first communion in May 1884. The album is illustrated with colored drawings of flowers, roses, violets, daisies, forget-me-nots, in profusion. Each page of the album represents a day, on which for two months Thérèse was to record the acts of virtue, love and sacrifice she practiced: the "flowers" offered each day to make her more worthy of receiving the Eucharist.

Once again, as the pretty album attests, Agnes and Thérèse are bound together as teacher and pupil. The hurt of Agnes's departure for the Carmel, without having informed her pupil of it, has healed. Many are the visits to Agnes in the speak room, many the intimate letters that fly between them. The album and Agnes's letters of those two months demonstrate the vigilance she exercised in her capacity as teacher. Both the album and the letters, moreover, point to a discovery surprising to this author.

The symbol of the flower that came to personify Thérèse was not of her invention. The use of flowers as symbols of love of God was introduced to her by Agnes. "Be brave in the planting of the flowers," her letters urge her pupil. "The garden [you] are preparing for Him will be more delightful than all of heaven's gardens."

Given such urgings and the pupil's tenacity, we find each page of the album painstakingly inscribed with the number of her offerings for the day. The grand total over two months reaches the staggering sum of 1,949 acts of virtue, love and sacrifice.

In future years, of course, she would seek to hide the virtues she possessed. She would disclaim any merits of her own, attributing them to Jesus, who bestowed them on her.

On May 4, 1884, when Thérèse was eleven, she made her first communion at the Benedictine Abbey. The solemn occasion was preceded by a three-day retreat with her classmates at the school. She was still the loner among them, without friends, and no less vulnerable to the sting of rejection. Despite her staggering number of acts of virtue, she was afflicted by scruples, that is, an exaggerated notion of having committed sin by the slightest offense. Chronic headaches still plagued her intermittently, symptoms of neurosis.

As the longed-for day approached, it seemed as if the above impediments were pitted against her tremendous desire to obtain to the fullest the sacramental grace the Eucharist would confer on her.

In quoting her account of that memorable day, we should keep in mind that it is Thérèse, the Carmelite nun, far advanced in her spiritual quest, who is looking back at the child of eleven, kneeling in her white dress and veil at the altar rail in the chapel of the Abbey, as the priest pauses before her in the white line of girls, the host upraised from his chalice.

It is in the language of the nun, not of the child, that she writes of that rapturous moment: "Ah, how sweet was that first kiss of Jesus. It was a kiss of *love!* I felt that I was *loved*; and I said [to him] 'I love You and I give myself to You forever.'" And she goes on in the rapture of the moment. "For a long time now Jesus and little Thérèse had looked at and understood each other. That day, it was no longer a *look*. It was a *fusion*. They were no longer *two*. Thérèse had vanished as a drop of water in the vastness of the ocean. Jesus alone remained. He was the Master, the King."

Carmel, the child felt more certain than ever, in the days that followed, was the desert where Jesus wished her to go hide herself. It was from then on the single objective of her life, not, as once it might have been, to be with Agnes again, but entirely for Jesus alone.

But there was still a giant leap the child must take, to be free of her impediments, a second miracle, as she called it.

It would be a grievous error to depict those two years as being of unrelieved gloom and misery for her. The sweet was mixed generously with the bitter, intervals of buoyant joy and pleasure, of inquisitiveness, the hunger to explore new horizons, typical of the preadolescent. She reveled in the annual summer vacation with the Guérins at Deauville and Trouville, climbing the steep cobbled streets of the hilly towns, watching the harbors as the fishing boats with their painted sails set out for the day's catch, and romping on the beach, hunting for seashells, enchanted by the blue immensity beyond the shore. At home, she and Céline were given drawing lessons, and both showed an aptitude for it, applying themselves to sketchbooks with enthusiasm. Her delight in nature was undiminished, evident in her sketches of animals, birds, trees and the inevitable flowers abloom on the paper.

Thérèse appropriated the attic at Les Buissonnets for her use as a retreat. Here is her description of how she fitted it out for herself: "It was a real bazaar, a collection of pious objects and curiosities, a garden and an aviary…A basket with pink ribbons contained delicate herbs and flowers…A little white desk held my schoolbooks and a statue of the Blessed Virgin…Upon a table was a large birdcage that enclosed a number of birds…Truly, this poor attic was a world to me."

She was an insatiable reader of books. Romantic legends of knights and chivalry, of kings and queens and noble heroes of history enthralled her. The person from history she most admired was Joan of Arc, savior of France, whose heroic exploits on the battlefield and in the court of the king she dreamed of emulating.

But dreams were only dreams, and not reality, and for her the bitter seldom lagged far behind the sweet.

By the winter of 1886, when Thérèse was thirteen, she seemed to have reached an impasse in her life, unable to move forward, held back by her inability to let go of her childhood and its encumbrances. She was obliged to attend the Abbey without the support of Céline, who at seventeen had finished the curriculum. To face school alone each day was at too dear a cost to her emotional stability. The freezing, bone-numbing Norman winters had confined her to bed repeatedly with colds and bronchial ailments. The worried family letters of that winter mention a persistent hacking cough that would not respond to medication, perhaps indicating her weakening resistance to infection. Implicit in the letters is a growing concern about the family darling, who seemed to be strangely set apart from them. Who could forget the child's terrifying plunge into near insanity that only a miracle, the Virgin's smile, could cure? In February Louis Martin abruptly withdrew Thérèse from the Abbey, suggestive of his alarm at her weakening condition. Thérèse would study for some months with Mme. Papineau, a private tutor in town, and that would end her formal education.

The summer of 1886 provided a respite from her difficulties, a vacation at Trouville with the Guérins followed by the peaceful solitude of the attic, tending her plants and herbs and aviary of birds. Her father had given her a frisky spaniel, named Tom, to enliven the hours. But then in October change came again to the Martin family.

Suddenly, impulsively, Léonie, the misfit of the family, decided to enter the Convent of the Poor Clares in Alençon. It was a rash decision. Unable to adjust to the rigors of religious life, Léonie was back home by December, more than ever conscious of her inferiority. But also in October, Marie, the eldest of the girls, the guiding light since Pauline's departure, made a decision about her future. She had not considered herself a likely candidate for the Carmel, but on the advice of her spiritual director, Pére Pichon, a Jesuit active in the diocese, confessor of Céline and Thérèse, and friend of the family, Marie applied to and was accepted as a postulant by the superiors of the Carmel. For the second but not the last time, a daughter of the family stepped through the cloister door that shut behind her, taking her leave of the world.

Marie's departure was not the shock that Pauline's had been for Thérèse. On the contrary, it served to intensity her determination to follow suit, which in turn increased her frustration at her incapacity to do so.

Sometime between October and December Thérèse must have realized that, if there were an enemy, the dragon, as it were, to slay, it consisted of nothing other than her own flawed self. Yet how to accomplish the task?

On the eve of Christmas of that year, unexpectedly, the answer was presented to her.

It was the custom in France for Christmas gifts to be exchanged on New Year's Day. Tradition also prescribed that on Christmas Eve children should place their shoes on the chimney

hearth to be filled with little toys and candies and trinkets in celebration of the holiday.

Upon coming home with her papa and sisters from Midnight
Mass at St. Pierre, Thérèse eyed with keen anticipation her gift-
laden shoes on the hearth. She wondered if at thirteen she was too
old for such indulgence, but, well, she enjoyed being treated as the
baby of the family, despite her age, and why not, after all?

She hurried off with Céline, up the stairs to remove their hats
and coats. Louis Martin, meanwhile, stood at the hearth, frowning
at the shoes. Perhaps he was fatigued from the lengthy service at
church and by the late hour. When the two girls started back down
the stairs, Thérèse was stopped, as if slapped in the face, by her
Papa's comment about her.

"Thérèse ought to have outgrown this sort of thing," he com-
plained to Léonie, gesturing at the shoes. "Let's hope it will be for
the last time."

Impaled on the stairs, hurt to the quick by the criticism,
Thérèse was stunned at what she'd overheard. Céline, expecting the
usual flood of tears, tried to ward off the copious flow. "Don't go
down just yet," she whispered urgently. "You'll cry if you look at
your gifts in front of Father."

But this was not the same girl of a moment ago. A force, some
core of strength deep within her, had taken hold. This other girl did
not flinch, cower back, or burst into tears. Instead, she ran gaily
down the stairs and over to her father at the hearth. She knelt
before him and reached for her shoes, exclaiming over each gift
with such delight and spontaneity that she earned his beaming
approval.

The transforming change in the girl—the giant vaulting leap
from who she had been to who she had become—what explains it?

How had she contrived in that instant to snatch victory from the jaws of the defeat she was accustomed to experiencing?

Thérèse offers us her explanation of it. "I was really unbearable because of my extreme touchiness," she writes of herself at thirteen. "If I caused anyone some little trouble, even unwittingly, rather than not crying, which made matters worse, I cried like a Magdalene, and then I cried for having cried."

She was until that night a touchy, pampered child, willful and prey to neurosis, and afterward quite another person, one of strength and resolution. A miracle? No Virgin's statue smiled at her, but, yes, it was that. To believe in miracles is only to credit the magnificence of God, manifested on earth...the sun dancing in the sky...a star, contrary to the solar system, moving eastward in the firmament to shine over the stable in Bethlehem...a trickle of water in a barren cave in a garbage dump, to reveal the hidden springs of curing waters beneath. Less spectacular, no less phenomenal are the everyday miracles, a pouch of money found in an alley, enough to pay the rent, a busy intersection crossed at one corner instead of another, out of the path of a car speeding out of control—everyday miracles that daily pass unnoticed and unacknowledged and are repeated by the thousands.

Thérèse expressed no doubt of what had been accomplished in her on that long-ago night. "The work I was unable to do for ten years, ever since I was four," she writes, "was done by God in one instant."

She refers, of course, to her thwarted attempts to correct her faults, accomplished by God in one transforming moment in her soul.

She was, indeed, as her family had sensed, set apart from the rest of us. That night she had left behind her the infirmities of her childhood. Yet always she would retain the glowing memory of her earliest years, of the child who had blossomed in the perfect love and trust of God and her family. It would be this image of the child that would form the imperishable doctrine that is her legacy to us.

From that night on onward, her trust in God, personified for her in Jesus, her guide and teacher, was complete and irrevocable. She was, moreover, fully resolved to enter the Carmel, where he wished her to be, at the latest by the next Christmas.

And should there be obstacles to prevent her from achieving her goal, she would overcome them.

8.

As the new year of 1887 dawned, and with it her fourteenth birthday, Thérèse looked forward with confidence to what in her mind would be its climax, her entrance into the Carmel, and she devoted her days to preparing herself for that event.

At fourteen, ripening into young womanhood, Thérèse had grown taller. The quiet composure that had not always been her prerogative made her seem older than her years. A vulnerability, a quickness to tears, still characterized her, but she was no longer helpless in dealing with it. From what she tells us of her prayers and reflections, a new consciousness was forming in her of what her life's mission was to be.

- "I felt charity enter my soul, and the need to forget myself and to please others."

- "I wanted to love, to love Jesus with a passion, giving Him a thousand proofs of my love."

- "I experienced a great desire to work for the conversion of sinners."

• "The cry of Jesus on the Cross sounded continually in my heart: 'I thirst.' I wanted to give my Beloved to drink, and I felt myself consumed with a thirst for souls."

To rescue sinners, to beg God's mercy for them, and to lead them to grace, out of love, would be her mission, and she pronounced herself ready to embark on that road.

There was good reason for Thérèse to feel confident in winning her goal of next Christmas. In her visits to the Carmel, weekly, except for Lent, when visits were not permitted, she had gained the unconditional support of Agnes. Since the age of nine, she'd been visiting the monastery regularly and was esteemed by the nuns almost as their protégée. More important, the prioress, whose approval was essential to her plan, doted on her. Mother de Gonzague, already a controversial figure in our story, was fully persuaded to accept the fourteen year old into the community as a postulant, and therein would complications arise. No convent is without its discreet game of politics, either among the nuns or in their opposition to the priests appointed to supervise them. In the case of Thérèse, the game would backfire for the nuns.

But that reversal had yet to occur, and Thérèse at the moment was concerned with obtaining her father's consent for her departure from home. She was his abiding joy, and he was revered by her, a precious token of her love. To renounce her life with him would be stressful and emotionally devastating for both. As her account of it makes clear, her dread at confronting him was absolved by his response to her plea.

It was spring by then, and the timing was less than propitious. Louis Martin was recovering from a slight paralytic stroke he had recently suffered. He was, at sixty-four, stooped and infirm, weighed down by abstractions, aged beyond his years. Thérèse was indispensable to such happiness as had accrued to him. She would not forget the frightening child's vision she'd had of her father, stumbling dazedly in the garden, a queer cloth thrown over his head, as if in prediction of some dire fate that awaited him, which she was powerless to prevent.

Still, God had willed Carmel for her, and she must obey his summons. The tender scene she describes is set in that same garden of her terrifying vision, appropriately at twilight of a tranquil Sunday evening in May. Father and daughter are alone together when she tells him of her plan to enter the Carmel and asks for his consent. Tears are shed by both, but Louis does not utter a word of protest. He is content merely to caution her as to the seriousness of her choice. And then, going over to the garden wall, "he pointed to some little white flowers, and plucking one of them, gave it to me," in a gesture to indicate his consent. Thus appears in the narrative the allusion to herself as a flower that will permeate the text.

Thérèse kept the white flower and noticed afterward that the stem was pulled out with the roots intact. It signified to her that her transplanting to the soil of Carmel would be made without breakage, intact.

There was reason for her confidence. In the person of her father she would find, despite his failing health, his preference for solitude, his withdrawal from the world, a staunch and vigorous advocate. Always a remote and distant figure on the periphery of our story, Louis Martin would acquire in the months ahead a size, a definition, that previously were not available to him.

The spring passed into summer, and she spent a week at Trouville with the Guérins, her last visit ever to the seashore. Back home again, she read in July of a local murder trial that set her upon a crusade.

Louis Martin did not allow the distraction of newspapers in the house. *La Croix*, a Catholic weekly, was the sole exception. In its pages Thérèse read of Pranzini, the murderer, on trial, who in August, defiant and unrepentant, had been judged guilty and condemned to the hangman's noose.

It seemed to Thérèse that the man was without someone to plead for God's mercy for him. She took on that task for herself and launched a crusade of prayer and Mass offerings to obtain mercy for him.

"I told God I was sure he would pardon the poor unfortunate Pranzini," she writes of her efforts. "I was absolutely confident of the mercy of Jesus, but I begged for a 'sign' of repentance, to give me courage to pray for sinners."

The date for the execution was August 31. All that month Thérèse pressed on with her vigil of prayers and Masses. Were she to be denied the sign she'd asked for, it would make no difference. She would still believe that Jesus in his mercy had forgiven the condemned man.

She read of the execution a day later in *La Croix*. Pranzini, showing no remorse for his crime, had climbed the steps of the gallows. A moment before the noose was slipped over his head, he had seized the chaplain's crucifix, lifted it to his lips and had kissed the corpus, after which the execution proceeded to its conclusion.

The condemned man would become, as she later referred to him, the first of her rescued "children," in her mission in behalf of sinners.

After such a victory, what could her confidence do but soar to the heights? Her entrance into Carmel was set for Christmas, a few short months away. Ah, there was no hardship, only ecstasy in waiting.

Unbeknown to Thérèse, a storm cloud was gathering over the Carmel. Although her entrance was set for Christmas, Mother de Gonzague, the prioress, had yet to inform the father superior, Canon Delatroette, whose approval was required in the matter. Rather than risk his refusal, which was likely, the nuns were playing a game of delay, stalling until it was too late for him to do other than decently give his approval. Should he refuse, the prioress was ready to appeal to the bishop to countermand him. When inadvertently he learned of all this, the elderly canon was furious. What, approve of the entrance of a child of fourteen? The nuns must be mad to think of it. In a thunderclap of anger and resentment, the canon declared that never, never would he approve of such a step. Adamant in his stand, he would not listen to the intercessions of the nuns. The storm cloud broke over the monastery in gale force.

And so, in the last days of October, a letter from a distraught Sister Agnes advised Thérèse of the canon's decision barring her entrance.

It would be supposed, given her vulnerability, that Thérèse would have been crushed by the news. Nothing of the kind. Jesus was her sponsor, and defeat was no longer in her vocabulary. She requested at once an interview with Canon Delatroette, and when he again refused to alter his decision, undeterred by her failure, and in consultation with her father, she asked that a meeting be arranged with the bishop of the home diocese of Bayeux, to present her cause to him.

There were other anxieties at home. In July, Léonie had impetuously left home and hearth to seek again a religious life with the Visitation nuns in Caen. The family worried that Léonie, so lacking in self-worth, so easily discouraged, would repeat her failure with the Poor Clares and return home once more. In six months, in fact, that is what she would do.

If the specter of failure loomed over the meeting with Bishop Hugonin, which has been duly arranged, Thérèse was undismayed by it. Jesus wanted her in the Carmel, and he would not be refused—it was as simple as that. Moreover, she already intended, should she fail, to appeal to a higher authority in the church.

On October 31 she departed by train for Bayeux, accompanied by her father. She'd put up her hair for the meeting to make herself appear older. There is a photograph of her, taken at the time, wearing a prim, high-necked dress and her new coiffure. The washerwoman's top knot of hair is clumsy and unattractive, but what magnetizes us in the photograph, apart from the clear gaze of her eyes and the shy tentative smile, is the firm thrust of her jaw, set in determination. It bespeaks of the strength in her character, the forged steel blade of her overwhelming power of will.

It was raining in Bayeux, a pelting, drenching rain that mingled with her tears of apprehension at having to confront the bishop. Nevertheless, as she blithely assures us, "I have observed in every crisis of my life that nature always reflected the image of my soul. On days filled with tears, the heavens cried along with me; in days of joy the sun beamed…and the blue skies were not obscured by a single cloud."

The meeting with Bishop Hugonin, and his vicar, Father Révérony, proceeded smoothly enough, but the conclusion was not what she'd hoped for. While the bishop was gracious in listening to her appeal, he would not countermand the canon's edict. No, Thérèse must wait some years before she might enter Carmel.

It would be thought that such a resounding defeat would have overwhelmed her, and tears aplenty were shed over it, but her mind was racing ahead to the next objective on the agenda. What if, she inquired of Hugonin...what if she were to obtain the pope's consent to her plea...would the bishop relent in his refusal?

The bishop's reply was noncommittal, and at that Louis Martin spoke up in behalf of his daughter. He was prepared, had already made the reservations, he informed Bishop Hugonin, to take Thérèse on a pilgrimage to Rome, to appeal directly to the pope, should that be her last recourse.

And so this was not the end of her hopes or of her pleas.

9.

The reservations Louis had made were for a pilgrimage to Rome, sponsored by the dioceses of Bayeux, Coutance and Nants, in Normandy. It was organized to celebrate the golden jubilee of Pope Leo XIII's ordination to the priesthood and would include a private audience with the pontiff. Typically, while assigning a worthy cause to the tour, religious observation was not the only item on the itinerary.

On November 4, 1887, a special luxury train embarked with the pilgrims for Paris, the first stop on the itinerary. On board, in their private compartment, were Louis Martin and his two pretty teenage daughters. As the youngest members in the party, the inseparable Thérèse and Céline would attract much comment and attention, some of it to their detriment.

The passenger manifest listed a complement of 197 pilgrims, culled from the three dioceses. Among them were the rich and titled, bound for pleasure in the deluxe hotels and restaurants as well as for edification. Seventy-five priests were listed in the manifest. One of the number was Father Révérony, Bishop Hugonin's representative, whose presence on the journey would prove crucial to Thérèse's future.

The prevalence of so many priests traveling with her, freed of the usual restraints, on holiday, more or less, would be an eye-opener for Thérèse. It would prompt her to revise her child's estimate of them.

She had believed, as she tells us in her account of the pilgrimage, that the souls of priests were without exception as pure as crystal. It therefore puzzled her that the principal aim of Carmelite nuns was to pray for the salvation of priests. What, in view of such purity, such perfection, was there to pray for?

The pilgrimage, the daily contact with priests at liberty, out to enjoy themselves, soon dispensed Thérèse of her child's naivete. As tactfully as she can phrase it, she concludes by saying that priests, after all, are in need of her prayers.

In Paris, between the rounds of sightseeing and shopping, Thérèse visited the Church of Our Lady of Victories, ever mindful of the statue at home that had smiled at the afflicted child and cured her of her illness. Ever single-minded, her prayers that day in church were for our Lady's help in the sole purpose of the journey, the audience with the pope, on which all of her anxious hope was pinned.

The chapter of the autobiography given to the pilgrimage is disappointing to the critical eye. The chapter reads like the journal of a teenage girl, which, of course, she was at the time, but one of no particular perception or discrimination. She "ohs" and "ahs" at the scenic wonders of Switzerland, the canals of Venice, the blue of the Bay of Naples, and acclaims with praise every religious shrine and edifice, every tomb and monument encountered on the tour. And while she mentions her apprehension as the tour moved on to its fateful climax in Rome, she fails to convey to the reader any real sense of what must have been her desperate urgency at the outcome.

For the pope was, indeed, the last card in her deck of dwindling options.

A fuselage of letters awaited Thérèse at each stop on the itinerary, filled with conflicting advice. The pilgrims had been instructed not to speak to the pope, but should she obey that stricture or not? Yes, she should, no, she should not, ran the advice. From the Carmel, Agnes recommended daring, having composed the exact petition to be addressed to the pope, while Marie sided with caution, and the prioress vacillated between the two poles. The Guérins were of mixed opinion, for and against Agnes's recommendation. To Céline, companion on the tour, in close proximity to her sister, the risk of speaking was eminently worth taking, the last desperate chance for Thérèse to win her goal of the Carmel by Christmas.

Neither Céline nor the letters seemed to give credence to the extreme shyness and timidity of a girl of fourteen, known to break into tears at the mere approach of a stranger.

So, then, there was high drama and suspense as the tour reached Rome and the day of the papal audience arrived, a day of reckoning for that girl.

On Sunday morning, November 20, 1887, the frail and aged Leo XIII celebrated Mass for the pilgrims in his private chapel in the Vatican. ("He's so old you'd say he was dead," was Thérèse's pithy appraisal of him.) Afterward, the pontiff, seated hunched over on a throne, received the pilgrims in an antechamber of the palace.

Father Révérony, who was in charge of protocol, stood at one side of the throne. The women were to be presented first, formed in a line, each dressed in the requisite black, floor-length gown and black lace mantilla. Each woman moved forward to kneel at the throne, kiss the papal ring and the scarlet papal slippers, be given a souvenir of the papal jubilee, and then in ceremonial order exit from the chamber. Father Révérony, concerned lest the pope become fatigued, had again forbidden that he be spoken to.

Thérèse and Céline stood toward the rear of the line of women, dressed in long black dresses and mantillas. Never before had Thérèse felt more conspicuous, more intimidated, more vulnerable to notice. As the line moved forward, and she advanced toward the throne, her courage was obviously faltering. *"Speak,"* Céline hissed at her from behind. But Thérèse appeared to be struck dumb, incapable of utterance. Then, having knelt and kissed the papal ring, speech came haltingly to her.

"Holy Father," she said, summoning what courage she could muster. "I have a great favor to ask of you…Holy Father, in honor of your jubilee, permit me to enter Carmel at the age of fifteen."

Révérony, aghast at her disobedience, quickly intervened. "This child's superiors, Your Holiness, are considering her request."

"Well, my child," the pontiff regarded the applicant, "do as your superiors tell you."

But Thérèse had unlocked a brave voice within her. She gripped the pope's knees urgently with her hands. "Oh! If only you would say, 'yes,' the others would agree," she pleaded.

Leo's response was not what she'd prayed to elicit from him. He gazed at her with furrowed brows, crouched on his throne, and then, slowly, solemnly stressing each word, spoke: *"Go…go,"* he said, dismissing her. *"You will enter…if God wills it."*

In a paroxysm of urgency, she would not give up her quest or, grasping onto the arms of the throne, her place at the pope's feet. The embarrassing spectacle went on, and then at a signal from Révérony, the papal guards removed the supplicant bodily from the chamber, to the shocked gasps of the onlookers. Her disgrace was complete.

A drama, or merely a tempest in a teapot? At stake was nothing more distressful then having to wait for permission to enter Carmel. For Thérèse, however, so ready and eager to do what she believed was God's will for her, the defeat in Rome was a calamity, as it was for Agnes and the nuns at Carmel enlisted in her support. Letters went back and forth, evaluating what, if anything, to do next. But as the tour moved on from Rome, there was a perceptible change in her outlook. She accepted the pope's verdict not as a defeat but as an expression of God's will, and thus accordingly was prepared to wait to accomplish her goal for as long as was required by her master.

And not all was lost on the tour. In the last days of the pilgrimage, Thérèse was elated to find a new defender, formerly an adversary, of her cause.

One afternoon, in the lovely hill town of Assisi, outside the Basilica of St. Francis, she was compelled to share a carriage ride back to the hotel with Father Révérony. He'd been observing her since Rome and was impressed by the quiet dignity of so young a person, and by the love she'd shown for her father. He felt sympathy for the desperation of her appeal to the pope, and what it must have cost her. No longer did her age seem to him a deterrent to her vocation. Before the carriage reached the hotel, chatting amiably with the girl, Father Révérony promised her that he would intercede for her with Bishop Hugonin, to obtain her goal.

The tour ended for the three Martins on December 2, 1887, with their return to Lisieux. Never again would there be the adventure of foreign lands for Thérèse, nor of any travel, never a step beyond the monastery walls. The greeting of Tom, her spaniel, the welcoming sight of Les Buissonnets, the gardens and fruit trees, stripped and bare, the attic made over into her aviary, was also a farewell to her home. In the same sense her reunion that evening with Agnes and Marie at the Carmel was a homecoming.

How long she must wait for Carmel was in God's hands, not hers. If it were not to be at Christmas, very well, it would at his discretion. Canon Delatroette was as opposed as ever to her entrance, but God would not keep her out. Meanwhile, in the time left to her in the world, she doubled her efforts to prepare herself for a life hidden from the world. From what she tells us of her efforts, it is not to be wondered at that she, who, in a flight of her spirit, had glimpsed the "T" of her name inscribed in the heavens, and whose message to us is all of love and forgiveness, should voice an aversion to cruel acts of mortification. Not for her the lash of the penitent's whip, the relentless scourging of the flesh. She sought instead simply to correct her faults, to leave behind her the spoiled family darling, and to curb the overwhelming power of her will.

"My mortifications," she tells us, "consisted in the breaking of my will, always so ready to impose itself on others, in holding back a reply, and in rendering little services to others without recognition."

So were spent the days of her waiting.

Christmas had come and gone, but three days later, on December 28, Mother de Gonzague, the prioress of Carmel, received a letter from Bishop Hugonin. Father Révérony's intercession had been effective. Overruling the canon's objections, the bishop gave his consent to the entrance of Thérèse Martin to the Carmel at Lisieux. The prioress, however, chose to delay her entrance. The season of Lent was approaching, rigorously observed by the nuns with fasting and other penances, and Mother de Gonzague felt rightly that the girl, still a child, really, should be spared those rigors and not enter until Lent was over in April.

A disappointment, surely, but having passed through a crucible of refusals, Thérèse was only momentarily disheartened by the news. Very well, since Jesus wished it, she would wait in patience and self-effacement.

No opposition, rebuff or refusal could have diverted her from her goal of Carmel, the absolute conviction that it was where Jesus wanted her to be. The urgency that underscored every move in her quest might be explained by what she tells of her sense, experienced earlier, that she was not destined for a long life. Time was therefore of the essence, not to be wasted.

The morning of April 9, 1888, at last arrived for her leave-taking from Les Buissonnets. She said goodbye to her childhood home with smiles, not tears, and a final hug for Tom, the spaniel, who had to be restrained from attempting to follow her through the gate. She made her last journey through the streets of Lisieux, accompanied by her father, Céline and Léonie, who was home by then from her failure with the Visitation nuns at Caen. The family group approached the gates of the monastery and filed through the gates to the chapel. A Mass of thanksgiving was celebrated for the family, after which Louis and his daughters proceeded to the cloister door for the last embraces, the last goodbyes.

The aspirant knelt for her father's blessing, which on his knees he gave to her. She stood before the door, on the other side of which her sisters, Agnes and Marie, the prioress and the community of nuns waited to receive her.

She stepped through the door, out of the world, Sister Thérèse of the Child Jesus, as henceforth she would be called, and the door closed irrevocably behind her for the fewer than ten years of life remaining for her.

PART FOUR

Birth of a Saint
1899–1925

*I considered that I was born for glory, and when
I searched out the means of acquiring it…God
made me understand that my own glory would
not be evident in the eyes of mortals, and that
it would consist of becoming a great saint.*

10.

In the town cemetery of Lisieux a cross in the long rows of crosses marked the freshly dug grave of the young nun who had died behind the walls of the monastery on the outskirts of town, a mysterious and forbidding place to the citizens who hastened by the gates. The aura of mystery made the young nun, in her brief and foreshortened life, hidden from the world, all the more unknown to the cemetery's visitors. It might be that the curious among them would linger for a moment at the gravesite to wonder about her fate. Here, beneath this cross, symbol of her life, she would lie in perpetuity, twice buried each winter by the snows, and that would be the end of her.

Except that it was not the end, but rather the beginning of her afterlife.

Already, even as the flowers on her grave withered and died, in a flutter of fallen petals, the young nun's destiny was stirring in the winds that swept over the cemetery...

Behind the walls of the Carmel, Mother Agnes was at work editing the manuscripts that Thérèse, before her death, had consigned to her care. She felt certain that publication would confirm her fierce, unyielding conviction that the manuscripts were the writings of a saint. To others of the nuns, there was a reverse factor to consider: Agnes, together with Sister Marie and Sister Géneviéve, who shared her convictions, were the older, adoring siblings of Sister Thérèse, which might be said to prejudice their lofty estimate of her virtues.

But no amount of dissent ruffled Agnes's composure, her sense of the rightness of her cause, as she assumed the labor of giving shape and unity to the disparate elements of the manuscripts.

It was to be a labor, it turned out, of herculean proportions, not all of it essential or required.

At her disposal, as Agnes proceeded to wield her editor's pen, were the two copybooks, the first of childhood memories, the second of life in the Carmel, that would comprise the principal text. A separate entity was the scrawled sheets of notepaper, written by Thérèse in the last weeks of her life, a manifesto of faith, that would need to be integrated into the text. There existed, in addition, a trove of materials to draw from in order to round out the book. Thérèse, the inveterate letter writer, had left copies of most of her letters, while her sisters and family members had preserved those addressed to them. And last, but not least, were the deathbed conversations faithfully recorded by her sisters in their journals.

Agnes's main effort as editor was to shape and organize the manuscripts into a unified, cohesive whole. She felt free to follow her own dictates in her capacity as editor. Thérèse, after all, had entrusted the manuscripts to her to make what changes were necessary for publication. It should be further noted that, even without this authorization, the Martin sisters were, as Thérèse's surviving siblings, the legal heirs to her property, to do as they wished with it.

However, rather than restrict her pen, Agnes imposed no limit on the changes she made as she worked on the manuscripts. This would later bring an avalanche of criticism upon her head.

Once again, it seems, Agnes was the teacher of former days, and Thérèse was her pupil, to be corrected accordingly. Agnes deleted passages in the manuscripts that she deemed inappropriate or trivial. (As one of her critics would later caution her, "Nothing in the life of a saint is trivial.") Other passages she rewrote entirely to conform to her ideas of discretion and propriety. Still others she enlarged to underscore and clarify the meanings. It was almost as if, in her zeal as editor, she had forgotten her own dazzling discovery of a saint in her sister's writings, to whom in sacred trust she had pledged her fealty and protection.

Before she was finished, Agnes was responsible for more than seven thousand deletions, transpositions, interpolations, corrections and additions to the manuscripts. The letters included in the final text, as well as the last conversations, were pruned and shorn of any references that Agnes worried might cause distress.

Yet, excessive as was her work as editor, was it also harmful and injurious to the manuscripts?

Not so many years later, Thérèse was not only a canonized saint but hailed by theologians for her doctrine of the "Little Way." Thanks to her writings, she had become, in today's parlance, a celebrity. Public clamor for the least scrap of information about her life was at its zenith. Thus, a light was brought on Agnes's contributions to the book that had made her sister world famous. In 1923, before the canonization, Pope Pius XI had appointed Agnes, as custodian of her sister's legacy, prioress for life of the Lisieux Carmel. It made her a fitting target to be attacked for having had the temerity to meddle in the work of a saint, and to be accused of dissembling in her altering of the text. She was unprepared for the boom of criticism that was lowered on her. In her mind, Agnes had done all she could to improve and enhance the manuscripts for publication, but evidently she had erred in her judgment. Slowly, painfully, over the years, while deploring that her sister in her grave was to be denied any vestige of privacy, Agnes bowed to the verdict of her critics, as she had once bowed to the demands of Mother de Gonzague, in order that a book might be born.

Agnes consented slowly to future editions of the unedited manuscripts, word for word, as written, and to separate volumes of the unedited letters and last conversations.

Today, when we read the manuscripts designated as A, B and C, exactly as Thérèse wrote them, and then compare the text to Agnes's earlier versions, we find unexpectedly that she did nothing to mar or efface her sister's doctrine or her message to us. Agnes, as editor, was concerned primarily with style and not with substance. Never does she alter or deflect the undying message to us of love and trust in the mercies of our Lord, Jesus.

Harmful, injurious to that message? Not to any significant degree, in the opinion of this writer, and when we reflect that, without her, we would not possess this spiritual treasure, it nullifies the charges against her.

Mother Agnes, still the prioress, still her sister's custodian, died in the Lisieux Carmel in 1951, at the venerable age of ninety. It is to her that we owe the gift she made possible, the story of a Little White Flower of Jesus, and of all that has evolved from it.

11.

By March 1898 Agnes had completed her work as editor. It was time to take the first step to publication. A copy of the manuscript was submitted to Bishop Hugonin, of the Bayeux diocese, for without his sanction the book, according to church law, could not be published.

The first hurdle was cleared when the bishop affixed his seal to the manuscript. Time to clear the next hurdle, finding a press to turn out the printed copies.

Since there was no publisher to assume the cost of printing, how was it to be paid for? The Lisieux Carmel, whose limited funds were usually near to depletion, was an unlikely source of money. The person credited with getting the book into print was none other than the author's uncle. Here again, in the history of the book, is an example of an individual who, with motives of his own at play, nevertheless, without knowing it, performed the work of Providence.

Isidore Guérin, forceful and arbitrary, owner of a pharmacy in Lisieux, was prominent in the Catholic life of the town. Beginning with his sister's marriage to Louis Martin, he had closely allied himself with the couple and their growing family. After Zélie's death, it was Isidore who had persuaded Louis to move with his five daughters from Alençon to Lisieux, where Mme. Guérin could provide the girls with a mother's care. From then on, Isidore kept a paternal eye on the girls' education and upbringing. Sundays for Louis and the girls were spent at the Guérins' home above the pharmacy. When Pauline, followed by Marie, entered the Carmel, it was not before each had obtained Isidore's gruff approval of the move. And next it was Thérèse's turn, trembling and timorous, to ask the same approval from her uncle. It was refused, and later given, the memory of which, years later, still left her quaking.

After Louis Martin's death, in 1894, Isidore became the head of the family, deferred to in his pronouncements. By then, too, his own daughter, Marie, wore the white veil of a novice in the Carmel, which deepened his relations with the nuns and his commitment to their welfare.

But was his commitment sufficient to take on the cost of printing his niece's book posthumously? He'd read the manuscript and strenuously objected to some of the content, which Agnes had then deleted or modified. While he loved Thérèse, in his gruff and blustering manner, no evidence suggests that he regarded either her or her book as exceptional in any sense whatever. Which brings us back to the question of why he underwrote the cost of publishing it.

It was most probably a matter to Isidore of family pride. His niece, a good and blameless little nun, had written a book and then had died. Isidore's opinion of the book wasn't the issue that concerned him. A member of the family had written a book, and who was to deny her the right to publish it? Not that he expected anything much to come of the book, but since Thérèse could not act on her own behalf, her family would act for her, a matter of pride, and help to get the book published.

That is one probable explanation for Isidore's paying the printing costs of the book.

Yet, all the while, it appears in retrospect, some other power was at work in Isidore Guérin, as it was in Agnes, with her zeal for publication, and in Mother de Gonzague, whose permission to publish was at least partly for the wrong reasons...all the while, these all too human beings were carrying out the will of God.

The search for a press was concluded, and in September 1898 a manuscript went off to the St. Paul Printing Co. in Bar-le-Duc. As the name implies, the company's business was the printing of Catholic materials.

At some undetermined point, a title was chosen for the book, borrowed from a line in the opening paragraph. It was to be called *The Story of a Soul,* or in French, *Histoire d'une Ame.*

The order from Lisieux was for a press run of two thousand copies. How the nuns must have fretted at the excessive number, fearing that the largest portion would wind up gathering dust on some storage shelf.

Bound copies of the book were delivered to the Lisieux Carmel, and on September 30, 1898, the first anniversary of the death of Thérèse, were sent as her obituary to the Houses of Carmel in France. Copies went out to Bishop Hugonin and his staff, to the Martin and Guérin families and their lists of friends, to the priests and nuns who had known or corresponded with the author, and to the friends and benefactors of the Lisieux Carmel.

It can be assumed that the most anxious party in this publishing venture of amateurs was Mother Agnes. As the mailings went out, and the book was read by her community of nuns, Agnes must have questioned whether her belief in the book's worth, her zeal in promoting it, would be justified by the response from its readers.

She could not have imagined, in her grandest expectations, the response of the public to *The Story of a Soul*. It was as if a match had been touched to kindling, igniting a flame that spread like wildfire throughout France, and then beyond it.

At the Carmel, and in rectories, convent parlors, and hearths and homes, in towns and cities and country villages in France, the book was read and eagerly passed from hand to hand in an ever-widening circumference of readers, many of whom rushed to the bookstores for their own copies, to be passed on accordingly. "I've just read the most wonderful book," the consensus seemed to chorus. "Here, I'll let you read my copy, but you'll want one of your own."

The Story of a Soul was from the outset the beneficiary of the most effective and powerful of any advertising medium: word of mouth, a giant engine that operated on its own power, full steam ahead, going wherever it chose to go, observing no boundaries or restrictions.

Within six months of publication, the first printing of the book was used up, exhausted. Copies were as scarce as hens' teeth to get hold of. A second printing of four thousand copies was run off at the St. Paul Press, and was likewise quickly exhausted in another few months.

And then, next, *The Story of a Soul* traveled beyond the boundaries of France. Over the next few years, editions of the book, licensed by the Lisieux Carmel, appeared throughout Europe, translated into German, Slovakian, Russian, Polish, Italian, Portuguese and Spanish. The English translation was a best seller in the British Isles. It would inspire in Ireland and Scotland two of the earliest shrines erected in honor of the author.

The book traveled across the Atlantic to the Americas, North and South, to Argentina, Brazil, Peru, Venezuela, to east and west of the Rockies in the United States, and north again to Canada and the provinces. The book crossed the Pacific to India, China, Japan, the Philippines, Australia, New Zealand. It rounded the Cape to Africa, a book that transcended the divisions of race, religions, cultures, possessed of a universal appeal.

And for the author of *The Story of a Soul*, who had never intended to write a book, and, dying, was unable to finish it, there arose a chorus of voices, among the multitudes of readers, proclaiming her to be one of God's chosen saints.

As early as 1902, visitors were arriving, unbidden, in Lisieux, to pray at the grave in the town cemetery, marked by a cross in the rows of crosses, swept by the winds and winter snows. By then, the Carmel was the daily recipient of hundreds of letters asking for mementoes, relics of the author. The volume of letters would swell into thousands each day, while at the monastery gates young women applied in the author's name for admittance as postulants.

It was not surprising, in view of the worldwide impact and influence of the book, that the church authorities in Rome should decide to look into the life and virtues of the author, in what would rapidly become the process of her canonization.

In 1910, the introduction of the cause of Sister Thérèse of the Child Jesus, deceased Carmelite nun, was announced in Rome. A diocesan tribunal was established in Bayeux, at which her writings were examined to determine the validity of the theology she had espoused. The tribunal summoned as witnesses the Martin sisters and family members, the nuns of the Carmel and those who had taught her at school, the priests who had been her confessors, the doctors who had attended her in her illness, the persons who had known or corresponded with her, to testify as to her character and sanctity.

Meanwhile, the body of Sister Thérèse was exhumed from the Lisieux cemetery, in its plain narrow pine coffin, and taken to a vault to await a final resting place.

In 1914, the Bayeux tribunal having favorably completed its investigation, a tribunal in Rome issued the formal *Approbation of the Writings*. Pope Pius XI then signed the *Decree for the Introduction of the Cause*. At this stage, as we have noted, the process could be terminated or stalled, sometimes for centuries of inquiry.

The cause of Sister Thérèse would be unprecedented in the swiftness by which it advanced to a conclusion. Yet, the tribunal in Rome, rather than praised for its expediency, might have been accused of lollygagging.

Even as the tribunal met in conference and summoned the parade of witnesses, the subject of the inquiry was already a national heroine of France and beloved by the world.

She was to her countrymen and women, up and down the length of, across the breadth of France, the Maid of Normandy, who by acclamation stood shoulder to shoulder with that other immortal heroine, the Maid of Orleans. The year, 1914, of the tribunal's investigation, was also the year that plunged Europe into World War I. As the war devastated France and drained the lifeblood of her young men, Thérèse was looked upon as a savior. Soldiers on the eve of combat prayed to her to protect them on the battlefield. Lying wounded in the trenches, the field hospitals, young soldiers near death invoked her name, entrusting to her their deliverance to heaven.

There was no dimming the light of her reputation as a savior of souls, she who had wished to spend her heaven in doing good on earth.

"When you get to heaven," her sisters, who nursed her in her illness, would jest with her, "will you look down on us?"

"No, I will come down," Thérèse had replied, in perfect earnestness. "I will return."

To the multitudes who believed in her, in France and beyond, it appeared that her prophecy had been realized, long before the church formally acknowledged it.

In 1923, the beatification of Sister Thérèse was celebrated by Pius XI in St. Peter's in Rome. Two years later, in 1925, he presided over the glittering ceremonies of her canonization.

The event, so long anticipated, indeed, demanded by her advocates, would seem to have brought closure to the public's clamor for her recognition. Instead, on the contrary, it unloosed the floodgates of the world's devotion to the fledgling saint.

Churches, schools, orphanages, missions, societies in every corner of the globe were named for her, and for the Little Flower, whose image she had taken for her own. Infant girls around the world were given the name of Thérèse in baptism. Statues of the saint were a fixture in the churches of five continents. Medals struck with her likeness, novena pamphlets to obtain her intercession, biographies, coloring books depicting her life, were for sale in religious-goods shops of many continents. Shrines were erected in her honor, near and far, in Kenya, Botsoland, the Fiji Islands, Indochina, Alaska, in Texas, Michigan and Illinois. The town of Lisieux, her girlhood home, the churches where she had worshiped, the monastery where she had lived and died in obscurity had become shrines, visited, as was the modest house of her birth in Alençon, by thousands each year.

It was a phenomenon unprecedented in the annals of the church, the tribute the world accorded to her in the years immediately following her canonization.

In 1927, Pius XI, calling her the greatest saint of modern times, designated Thérèse to be the co-patron, with St. Francis Xavier, of all the missions and missionaries, men and women, that encompassed the globe. Ironically, her great desire to be a missionary in foreign lands had been unfulfilled, thwarted by her illness and death. Later, Thérèse would be honored as the co-patron, with Joan of Arc, of France, and her protection would be sought again by soldiers in the Second World War. By decree of Rome, a magnificent basilica would rise on a hilltop in Lisieux, the final resting place of her mortal remains.

And all of it, the honors, the acclamations, the unprecedented world veneration of her, were the direct outcome of a book she had never set out to write, left unfinished at her death, and which was published by amateurs as her obituary.

Few knowledgeable persons would have accorded the book any chance for success, and yet it had traveled the world, to the most distant outposts, to the most intense, deeply felt response of its polyglot readers, who adopted it and the author for their own. Why? What explains the phenomenon?

What explains the universal appeal of *The Story of a Soul?*

By the 1930s, over five million copies of the little book, in various editions, translated into thirty-five languages, were in worldwide circulation. Here, uniquely, was a book that had launched the author like a blazing rocket into the orbit of universal saints, earning for her the world's devotion.

A similar response, some years later, was accorded to the publication of *The Diary of Anne Frank*. The two books share a number of similarities. Each was the work of a very young woman, unknown to the world, who had no thought of future publication. Each wrote from the perspective of a restricted life, one having chosen the prison of a monastery, the other having to live in fear in the prison of the attic imposed on her: her family's hideout from Nazi persecution of the Jews in World War II. Yet each espoused a doctrine of hope and the ultimate salvation of the human spirit from annihilation. Some critics have interpreted a darker meaning in the diary, but the majority holds it to be a testament of faith in the goodness of life, which surely is the message of *The Story of a Soul*.

Not every reader, of course, experienced the same ecstatic response to the book. For them, as it was initially for me, the book was overly sweet and sentimental, sticky sweet and cloying, to the degree that I put the book aside without having finished it.

Years later, I again picked up a copy of *The Story of a Soul*. The experience of reading it again, not for style but for substance, was transcendental. I found it to be one of the great books of Christian literature. I was no longer young by then, with the arrogance of the young. Old age and its penalties were not that far off on the horizon. I needed some affirmation of what I believed to be the reason for living, for getting on with the daily business of life, rather than to fall behind at the wayside of despair.

All of this, and more, did I find in *The Story of a Soul*. If this book of mine serves a purpose, it is to call attention to that other account of a life that has yielded such riches in my life.

The epochal spiritual journey made by Thérèse is best told, not in my words, but in her words. And so what follows in the next part of this book is a kind of compendium of her thoughts and aspirations, ending with her last magnificent testaments of faith, as told by her.

She sought to be little, rather than big, to be poor, not rich, and to be last instead of first in her quest to serve God and not herself.

Which is to say that St. Thérèse sought the very opposite of what so many of us seek from life, never more so than in this day and age. Consider for a moment what it entails to choose to be last in the line pushing and shoving to get onto a crowded bus. What if the bus is full before you can board it, and the doors snap shut in your face? Must you again choose to be last in the line that quickly forms for the next bus? Yes, you must, if you are true to your avowals. Such hard choices were made by Thérèse again and again, day in and day out of her life. It became in her a perfect expression of the Christian ideals of humility and love of neighbor, rather than of self.

And she did all this in total obscurity, careful that her efforts should pass unnoticed.

Thérèse dreamed of performing grand acts of heroism for God, but the life she was given was not a canvas painted on a grand scale. It was instead a miniature, made up of the ordinary, the joys and sorrows, the failings and discouragements, the trials and tribulations common to all of us. The difference was that the ordinary became her rallying cry. Her "littleness" was the banner she carried onto the battlefield, in the war she waged in behalf of love versus selfishness, of hope rather than despair, of forgiveness instead of vengeance, the prizes ready to be won in our daily battles with ourselves.

In striving always to be little and poor, the last in the line, Thérèse raised up the ordinary to the heroic level that made her a saint. From her hidden practice of virtue, she evolved a doctrine, startlingly original, of a new way for the millions of us, little like her, though not from choice, to live out our lives in accordance with God's intentions for us.

It amounted to nothing less than a doctrine of liberation, taking us beyond our faults and limitations into a whole new realm of possibilities.

We need not wonder how she accomplished so much in so short and restricted a life, shut away from the world, yet with an acute intuitive sense of its beauties, vanities and seductions. Thérèse herself has told us of the journey she embarked on, charting each step of the course. *The Story of a Soul*, presented in its original form, is still the richest source of information and enlightenment of her life.

We have already summarized the astonishing history of the publication of *The Story of a Soul*—its rocket-like ascent into the ranks of worldwide best sellers, translated into multiple languages, read and read again by millions.

But what of the contents that enthralled its readers and led eventually, beyond the author's canonization, to her designation by Pope John Paul II as a doctor of the church, only the third woman in church history thus to be honored.

Really, a book of its own is needed to do justice to the spiritual benefits to be drawn from a detailed study with commentary of the text, to serve as a daily source of reflection and meditation.

However, owing to the limits of space, we must be content to present the reader with what are acknowledged by theologians as two of the most profound and stirring passages of the text, which together compose a beautiful and luminous treatise on the theme of Christian love.

Here, then, is Thérèse, in her own words, speaking in her own inimitable voice.

Each passage is prefaced by a commentary that tells the background and circumstances of the writing.

PART FIVE

In Her Own Words
1895–1897

God made me always desire what
He wanted to give me.

12.

The forces that were shaping the destiny of Sister Thérèse of the Child Jesus moved swiftly and decisively in the year 1896. The events of that year suggest that sometimes it is by trial and tribulation that God manifests his will for us.

In March 1896 the election of a prioress came due again at the Carmel. Mother Agnes of Jesus had served out her three-year term of office, during which she had commanded Thérèse to write her childhood memories. Two months before the election, in January, Thérèse had submitted the first of what were to be three manuscripts of her story. Dazzled by what she read, Agnes was convinced that she had to advance the continuation of the work, which she viewed as her life's mission.

Unfortunately, after the March elections, Agnes was no longer in a position to issue commands. She had lost her bid for a second term, in what must have seemed evidence of the nuns' displeasure with her. Agnes was plagued with doubt that the saint's testimony, as she saw it, would ever be finished or given to the world.

A month after the election, in April 1896, another devastating blow was dealt the future of the book. On the morning of Good Friday, Thérèse awoke in her cell, a hemorrhage of blood gushing from her mouth. It was the first sign of the fatal disease that would claim her life before the next year's terminus. What for us would have been, understandably, a dark and terrifying event, was not so for Thérèse. The attainment of heaven had been her goal for almost her entire life, and now she had heard "the first sweet call of the Bridegroom." Her only concern was to be able to carry on her duties, the teaching of the novices, the work on the manuscript. That morning, with that objective, she reported the hemorrhage to the prioress, as the Rule required, and asked for permission to go on with her duties as before.

Permission was granted.

A rash consent, perhaps. If one examines the photographs of Thérèse onward from 1896—the puffy eyes rimmed by shadows, the pallor, the sense of ebbing strength in her posture, the exhaustion of posing for the camera—there are indications of a precipitous decline in her health. Yet she was granted permission to stagger on with her work. Who could have been so blind or insensitive to another's failing condition? Why was the prioress so careless of someone in her charge?

Mother de Gonzague's one term out of office had left her restless and dissatisfied. To be in command she regarded as her natural prerogative. Thus, by the exercise of her guile and charm, her wiles and flattery, Gonzague had persuaded the necessary quota of nuns to return her to office. Eventually, she would serve six terms.

But was it cruel and unthinking of the prioress to permit a nun in serious ill-health to carry on, unrelieved, with her duties?

We are interested here less in the actions of individuals than in the action of God's will in the making of a saint.

From that vantage point, there is something to be said in defense of Mother de Gonzague. Despite her many outrageous faults, she was possessed of a sharp and penetrating intelligence, though often put to poor use. Not so in her treatment of Thérèse. More than anyone else at the Carmel, including Agnes, Mother de Gonzague understood perfectly the character of Thérèse. She was a rock, a fortress of spiritual strength, able to withstand attack from any quarter. Thérèse, Gonzague had once remarked, displayed every ideal quality for the office of prioress, despite her youth. Not from idle whim had she assigned Thérèse to the teaching of the novices. Who better to school them in the practice of virtue?

This rock, this fortress, asked, despite the alarming symptoms of disease, to go on with her duties, and Mother de Gonzague, knowing her capabilities, consented to it.

Trials and tribulations...

As the year 1896 wore on, Mother Agnes reappraised her own situation. All previous doubts were dispelled. The work of shaping the manuscripts into a book would go on. She would attend to it, herself at the helm. It might even be fortuitous, given the tremendous task ahead, that she had not been reelected prioress. Considering the demands of the office, how would she ever have found time to work on the book?

It was ironic that at this juncture of her resolve, the urgent need for Thérèse to continue her writing, the dip, dip, scratch, scratch of her pen, Agnes was confronted with the same dilemma as when she first conceived of the venture. It would again be necessary to gain the consent of her old adversary, the prioress, for the work to proceed.

The crisis was one that Agnes had solved before. Again swallowing her pride, Agnes took herself to the office of the prioress and begged that Thérèse be permitted to devote full time to her writing.

And as before, Mother de Gonzague consented to the plea, but with a stipulation. The next chapters must conform to the earlier pages, that is, they must be addressed personally to her, or she would withdraw her consent.

And so it was that Thérèse, in reaching again for her pen, the quick dip in the ink pot, addressed her first words of surpassing beauty to her prioress, not in the least distressed to do so.

The Elevator

"You have told me, my dear Mother, of your desire that I finish *singing* with you the *Mercies of the Lord*.

"You know, Mother, I have always wanted to be a saint. Alas! I have always noticed that when I compare myself to the saints, there is between them and me the same difference that exists between a mountain whose summit is lost in the clouds and the obscure grain of sand trampled underfoot by passers by. Instead of becoming discouraged, I said to myself: God cannot inspire unrealizable desires. I can, then, in spite of my littleness, aspire to holiness. It is impossible for me to grow up, and so I must bear with myself such as I am with all my imperfections. But I want to seek out a means of going to heaven by a little way, a way that is very straight, very short, and totally new.

"We are living now in an age of inventions, and we no longer have to take the trouble of climbing stairs, for, in the homes of the rich, an elevator has replaced these very successfully. I wanted to find an elevator which would raise me to Jesus, for I am too small to climb the rough stairway of perfection. I searched then, in the Scriptures, for some sign of this elevator, and I read these words coming from the mouth of Eternal Wisdom: *'Whoever is a LITTLE ONE, let him come to me.'* And so I succeeded. I felt I had found what I was looking for. But wanting to know, O my God, what You would do to the very little one who answered Your call, I continued my search and this is what I discovered: *'As one whom a mother caresses, so will I comfort you; you shall be carried at the breasts, and upon the knees they shall caress you'* Ah! never did words more tender and more melodious come to give joy to my soul.

"The elevator which must raise me to heaven is Your arms, O Jesus! And for this I had no need to grow up, but rather I had to remain *little* and become this more and more.

"Dear Mother, you know well that God has deigned to make me pass through many types of trial. I have suffered very much since I was on earth, but if in my childhood I suffered with sadness it is no longer in this way that I suffer. It is with joy and peace. Ah! if the trial I have suffered for a year now appeared to the eyes of anyone, what astonishment would be felt!

"At this time I was enjoying such a living faith, such a clear *faith*, that the thought of heaven made up all my happiness, and I was unable to believe there were really impious people who had no faith, and who, through the abuse of grace, lost this precious treasure. Then God permitted my soul to be invaded by the thickest darkness, and that the thought of heaven, up until then so sweet to me, be no longer anything but the cause of struggle and torment. This trial was to last not a few days or a few weeks; it was not to be extinguished until the hour set by God Himself and this hour has not yet come. One would have to travel through this dark tunnel in darkness. I will try to explain it by a comparison.

"I imagine I was born in a country that is covered in thick *fog*. I never had the experience of contemplating the joyful appearance of nature flooded and transformed by the brilliance of the sun. It is true that from childhood I heard people speak of these marvels, and I know the country I am living in is not really my true fatherland, and that there is another I must long for without ceasing. This is not simply a story invented by someone living in the sad country where I am, but it is a reality, for the King of the fatherland of the bright sun actually came and lived for thirty-three years in the land of darkness. Alas! the darkness did not understand that this Divine King was the Light of the world.

"Your child, however, O Lord, has understood Your divine light, and she begs pardon for her brothers. She is resigned to eat the bread of sorrow as long as You desire it; she does not wish to rise up from this table filled with bitterness at which poor sinners are eating until the day set by You. Can she not say in her name and in the name of her brothers, *'Have pity on us, O Lord, for we are poor sinners!'* Oh! Lord, send us away justified. May all those who were not enlightened by the bright flame of faith one day see it shine. O Jesus! if it is needful that the table soiled by them be purified by a soul who loves You, then I desire to eat this bread of trial at this table until it pleases You to bring me into Your bright Kingdom. The only grace I ask of You is that I never offend You!

"When I want to rest my heart fatigued by the darkness that surrounds it, it seems to me that the darkness, borrowing the voice of sinners, says mockingly to me: 'You are dreaming about the light, about a fatherland embalmed in the sweetest perfumes; you are dreaming about the *eternal* possession of the Creator of all these marvels; you believe that one day you will walk out of this fog that surrounds you! Advance, advance; rejoice in death which will give you not what you hope for but a night still more profound, the night of nothingness.

"I run toward my Jesus."

"I remember an act of charity God inspired me to perform while I was still a novice. It was only a very small thing, but *our Father who sees in secret* and who looks more upon the intention than upon the greatness of the act has already rewarded me without my having to wait for the next life.

"It was at the time Sister St. Pierre was still going to the choir and the refectory. She was placed in front of me during evening prayer. At ten minutes to six a Sister had to get up and lead her to the refectory, for the infirmarians had too many patients and were unable to attend to her. It cost me very much to offer myself for these little services because I knew it was not easy to please Sister St. Pierre. She was suffering very much and did not like it when her helpers were changed. However, I did not want to lose such a beautiful opportunity for exercising charity, remembering the words of Jesus: *'Whatever you do to the least of my brothers, you do to me.'* I offered myself very humbly to lead her, and it was with a great deal of trouble that I succeeded in having my services accepted!

"Each evening when I saw Sister St. Pierre shake her hourglass I knew this meant: Let's go! How difficult it was for me to get up, especially at the beginning; however, I did it at once, and then a ritual was set in motion. I had to remove and carry her bench in a certain way, above all, I was not to hurry as the walk took place. It was a question of following the poor invalid by holding her cincture. I did this with as much gentleness as possible. But if by mistake she took a false step, immediately it appeared to her that I was holding her incorrectly and that she was about to fall. 'Ah! my God. You are going too fast; I'm going to break something.' If I tried to go more slowly, 'Well, come on! I don't feel your hand; you've let me go and I'm going to fall! Ah! I was right when I said you were too young to help me.'

"Finally, we reached the refectory without mishap; and here other difficulties arose. I had to seat Sister St. Pierre and to act skillfully in order not to hurt her; then I had to turn back her sleeves (again in a certain way) after which I was free to leave. With her poor crippled hands she was trying to manage with her bread as well as she could. I soon noticed this, and each evening I did not leave her until I had rendered her this little service. As she had not asked for this, she was very much touched by my attention. It was by this means that I gained her entire good graces, and this especially (I learned later) because, after cutting her bread for her, I gave her my most beautiful smile before leaving her.

"One winter night I was carrying out my little duty as usual; it was cold; it was night. Suddenly, I heard off in the distance the harmonious sound of a musical instrument. I then pictured a well-lighted drawing room, brilliantly gilded, filled with elegantly dressed young ladies conversing together and conferring upon each other all sorts of compliments. Then my glance fell upon the poor invalid I was supporting. Instead of the beautiful strains of music I heard only her occasional complaints, and instead of the rich gildings I saw only the bricks of our austere cloister, hardly visible in the faintly glimmering light. I cannot express in words what happened in my soul; what I know is that the Lord illumined it with rays of *truth* which so surpassed the dark brilliance of earthly feasts that I could not believe my happiness. And I would not have exchanged the ten minutes employed in carrying out my humble office of charity to enjoy a thousand years of worldly feasts.

"What will this happiness be in heaven when one shall see in the midst of eternal joy and everlasting repose the incomparable grace the Lord gave us when He chose us *to dwell in His house*, heaven's real portal?"

13.

The scene, which we have visited once before in these pages, is the common room of the monastery. It is a wintry night in December

1895. The nuns are gathered for recreation, the one hour when silence is set aside for the pleasures of conversation. Off in a corner are seated together a little circle of four nuns. They are sisters in life as well as in religion. The youngest of the four is entertaining the others with humorous stories of their earlier life as a family at home. Her audience is captivated by her narrative, told with such verve and animation and peals of laughter.

The storyteller is, of course, Thérèse. The hour is fast winding down, but the foursome in the corner are in no hurry to end the dwindling hour. The blazing fire of logs shooting off sparks in the hearth explains the absence of haste in all of the nuns. The fire provides the one and only source of heat in the entire monastery, upstairs and down. The Rule that dictates the paucity of heat goes back to the 1500s, when the Reformed Order of Carmel was established in Spain. Since the climate there was mild and temperate— sunny Spain, after all—the Rule specified each house of the Order would be limited to one fire at night, as warmth against the chill, which was perfectly adequate. But when the growth of the Carmelite Order soon spread to France and northern Europe, the edict of one fire per house was left intact, despite the frigid winters of the north. In the 1890s it was still in effect, the cause of great hardship for the nuns. Thérèse suffered cruelly from the cold, almost to the point of death, she later testified. There is a photograph of her, taken in 1895. She is seated in a group of nuns. Her face, calm and composed, is puffy with illness. Her hands are folded in her lap, the fingers swollen to sausage size from chilblains. We can appreciate, therefore, how the nuns must have savored the last of the warmth as the hour of recreation drew to a close.

Before that moment, however, one of the nuns in the circle of four ventured to make a suggestion in regard to the storytelling.

"What a pity," sighed Sister Marie of the Sacred Heart, "that these wonderful stories are not preserved in writing. Think what a treasure of memories the family would have to share and enjoy."

Of a shy and hesitant nature—it cost her effort to speak out like that—Marie was the eldest of the Martin sisters. She was the second to enter Carmel, after Pauline, not from any strong sense of vocation, it would seem, but at the suggestion of her Jesuit confessor. She felt herself inadequate in her practice of religion, uninspired, of no spiritual insight, just one of the herd. Mother Agnes, in Marie's estimate, was a marvel of capability and command. Thérèse, at her entrance at fifteen, was still a child to Marie, much loved, but unschooled in the means of achieving spiritual perfection. This negative view was, in a short span of years, to change radically. In that short span, Thérèse's role as the baby of the family, to be petted and indulged, no longer existed. She was now the undisputed authority among her sisters on the practice of religion. The timid pupil had become the bold and daring teacher of new concepts of devotion to God. Marie, for her part, was the eager pupil, consulting the teacher for the answers to sanctity that had eluded her.

Marie was older than Thérèse by thirteen years. The relation between them was more that of a doting spinster aunt and her adored niece. She was lavish in expressing her love and praise of Thérèse in little notes slipped into her hand as she passed by her in silence in a corridor. The scene in the common room that December was typical of Marie's conduct in that regard.

But no one in all the wide world could have predicted the ultimate outcome of Marie's suggestion.

"What a pity that these wonderful stories are not preserved in writing. Think what a treasure of memories the family should have to share and enjoy."

Mother Agnes, quick to intuit opportunity, seized upon Marie's suggestion. She turned and ordered, as prioress, the startled Thérèse to set down her memories in pen and paper.

If not for Marie, would there have been a book to travel the world, inspiring millions? That question is answered by the instance of God having chosen Marie as the instrument to launch the epic journey.

All of which is simply to supply a background for what was to be another of Marie's requests. Such was the progress of Thérèse's illness, the invasion of tuberculosis in her system, draining away her energy, that by midyear of 1896 she had been relieved of her duties. To be useless, of no service to the life of the community, was a horror for her to contemplate. We already know how her inactivity was solved: Mother de Gonzague gave her permission to devote herself full time to the manuscripts. The dying young nun lay in bed (a straw pallet), writing board propped on her knees, pen dip-dipping into the ink pot, and worked to complete what she had begun so lightly, with no thought of its future journey.

A little note from Sister Marie, a timid request, slipped under the door of her cell, interrupted the flow of the pen. Thérèse had never failed to respond to these requests from her sister, nor did she turn away from this latest one. Her response would later be recognized as a masterpiece of Christian literature.

The Vocation

"You asked me, dear Sister, to write to you of 'my little doctrine' as you call it. Ah! if all weak and imperfect souls felt what the least of souls feels, that is, the soul of your little Thérèse, not one would despair of reaching the summit of the mount of love. Jesus does not demand great actions from us, but simply surrender and gratitude.

"When writing these words, I shall address them to Jesus, since this makes it easier for me to express my thoughts, but it does not prevent them from being very poorly expressed.

"O Jesus, my Beloved, to be Your Spouse, to be a Carmelite, and by my union with You to be the Mother of souls—should this not suffice me? And yet it is not so. I feel within me other vocations. I feel the vocation of the WARRIOR, THE PRIEST, THE APOSTLE, THE DOCTOR, THE MARTYR. Finally, I feel the need and desire of carrying out the most heroic deeds for You, Jesus. I feel within my soul the courage of the Crusader, and I would want to die on the field of battle in defense of the Church.

"I feel in me the vocation of the PRIEST. With what love, O Jesus, I would carry You in my hands when, at my voice, You would come down from heaven. And with what love would I give You to souls. But alas! while desiring to be a Priest, I admire and envy the humility of St. Francis of Assisi in refusing the sublime dignity of the Priesthood.

"O Jesus, my Love, my Life, how can I combine these contrasts? How can I realize the desires of my poor little soul?

"Ah! in spite of my littleness, I would like to enlighten souls as did the Prophets and the Doctors. I have the vocation of the Apostle. I would like to travel over the whole earth to preach Your Name and to plant your glorious Cross on infidel soil. But O My Beloved, one mission alone would not be sufficient for me. I would want to preach the Gospel on all the five continents simultaneously, even to the most remote isles. I would be a missionary, not for a few years only, but from the beginning of creation until the consummation of the ages.

But above all, O my beloved Savior, I would shed my blood for You even to the very last drop.

"O my Jesus! what is Your answer to all my follies? Is there a soul more little, more powerless than mine? Nevertheless, even because of my weakness, it has pleased You, O Lord, to grant my little childish desires, and You desire to grant other desires that are greater than the universe.

"During my meditation, my desires caused me a veritable martyrdom, and I opened the Epistles of St. Paul to find some kind of answer. Chapters 12 and 13 of the First Epistle to the Corinthians fell under my eyes. I read there, in the first of these chapters, that all cannot be apostles, prophets, doctors, etc., that the body of the Church is composed of different members, and that the eye cannot be the hand at one and the same time. The answer was clear, but it did not fulfill my desires and gave me no peace. Without becoming discouraged, I continued my reading, and this sentence consoled me: *'Yet strive after THE BETTER GIFTS, and I point out to you a yet more perfect way.'* And the Apostle explains how all the most perfect gifts are nothing without *LOVE*. That Charity is the EXCELLENT WAY that leads most surely to God.

"I finally had rest. Considering the mystical body of the Church, I had not recognized myself in any of the members described by St. Paul, or rather I desired to see myself in them *all*. Charity gave me the key to my vocation. I understood that if the Church had a body composed of different members, the most necessary and most noble of all could not be lacking to it, and so I understood that the Church *had a Heart and that this Heart was BURNING WITH LOVE. I understood it was Love alone* that made the Church's members function, that if Love ever became extinct, apostles would not preach the Gospel and martyrs would not shed

their blood. I understood that LOVE COMPRISED ALL VOCA-
TIONS, THAT LOVE WAS EVERYTHING, THAT IT
EMBRACED ALL TIMES AND PLACES…IN A WORD,
THAT IT WAS ETERNAL!

"Then, in the excess of my delirious joy, I cried out: O Jesus,
my Love…my *vocation*, at last I have found it…MY VOCATION
IS LOVE!

"Yes, I have found my place in the Church and it is You, O my
God, who have given me this place; IN THE HEART OF THE
CHURCH, I SHALL BE LOVE. THUS I SHALL BE EVERY-
THING, AND THUS MY DREAM WILL BE REALIZED.

"O Jesus, I know it, love is repaid by love alone.

"I am a child, and the heart of a child does not seek riches and
glory (not even the glory of Heaven). What this child asks for is
Love. But how will she prove her *love,* since love is proved by
works. Well, the little child *will strew* flowers, she will perfume the
royal throne with *sweet scents*, and she will sing in her silvery tones
the canticle of *Love*.

"Yes, my Beloved, this is how my life will be consumed. I have
no other means of proving my love for you other than that of strew-
ing flowers, that is, not allowing one little sacrifice to escape, not
one look, one word, profiting by all the smallest things and doing
them through love; and in this way I shall strew flowers before
Your throne. I shall sing, even when I must gather my flowers in
the midst of thorns, and my song will be all the more melodious in
proportion to the length and sharpness of the thorns.

"O Jesus! Why can't I tell all *little souls* how unspeakable is
Your condescension? I feel that if You found a soul weaker than
mine, You would be pleased to grant it still greater favors, provided

it abandoned itself with total confidence to Your Infinite Mercy. But why do I desire to communicate Your secrets of Love, O Jesus, for was it not You alone who taught them to me, and can You not reveal them to others? Yes, I know it, and I beg You to cast Your glance upon a great number of little souls worthy of Your love."

(signed)   The very little Thérèse of the Child Jesus and the Holy Face, unworthy Carmelite religious.

Death—"the Thief," she calls it—is stealing ever closer to her bed, but still she goes on:

"Since Jesus has reascended into heaven, I can follow him only in the traces He has left, but how luminous these traces are! how perfumed. I have only to cast a glance at the Gospels and I immediately breathe in the perfumes of Jesus' life, and I know on which side to run. I don't hasten to the first place but to the last; rather than advance like the Pharisee, I repeat with confidence the publican's humble prayer. Yes, I feel it, even though I had on my conscience all the sins that can be committed, I would go, my heart broken with sorrow, and throw myself into Jesus' arms, for I know how much He loves the prodigal child who returns to Him. It is not because God, in His anticipating Mercy, has preserved my soul from mortal sin that I go to Him with confidence and love..."

With the last sentence left unfinished, Thérèse has come to the end of the story of her soul. The pencil—she is too worn down for pen and ink—drops from her hand. It is July 1897. She sinks back on the pillow of her bed in the infirmary, attended by her three devoted sisters. Each is keeping a record of her conversations with them—*"When you get to Heaven, will you look down on us?" "No, I will come down. I will return"*—a chronicle of her last months on this earth. Agnes, ever the guardian, will complete the editing of the manuscripts and attend to the little book's publication.

It is July, but not for another sweltering, agonizing two months, on the evening of September 30, at seven o'clock, will Thérèse end her journey here below, flying to her Jesus in heaven and into her glory.

And so in these pages we leave her as we first encountered her, on her deathbed, unknown to the world, shut away from the world, yet embarked on her mission of making souls love God as she loved him, by her Little Way of helping all of us, despite our flaws and errors and wrong turns in the road, to become heaven bound, too.

The Saint Who Loved Us
1999

October 1999

A couple of years ago, I would have walked the short distance from Second Avenue, but here I was, like the old man I was, riding the few blocks on the 23rd St. crosstown bus, the better to conserve my flagging energy.

But this was a holiday for me, away from my typewriter—yes, I still use that antiquated machine—and I felt a lively spring to my step as I got off the bus at Park Avenue South. It used to be called Fourth Avenue and evoked memories for me of the secondhand bookstores, the happy browsing among the dusty stacks, that populated a few blocks below 14th Street. It's that way for me all over New York, vanished landmarks, the former sites of which, glimpsed from a bus, send me on journeys down memory lane.

You might say that today was such a journey for me, I speculated, waiting for the light to go red on Park. I'd been working on a book, sweating it out, for two years by now. It wasn't another novel but a book about…well, about the life and death of a saint. I didn't write biographies, and God knows I wasn't a theologian or authority on the psychology of saints. I was riddled with doubts that I could bring it off, and couldn't think why I'd taken it on. Oh, yes, I could…

And today, I would be revisiting a long-ago scene from my past, Paris, World War II, where perhaps the subject of my book had announced herself to me, eventually to become a part of my life.

So, in that sense, today wasn't entirely a holiday for me but a somber remembrance.

The green light flicked to red, and I hurried in the stream of pedestrians across the four lanes of halted traffic on Park. I aimed for the bus stop at the opposite corner, fretting, to my annoyance, about the book.

The sparkle in the air, the lingering summer warmth mixed with the crisp, cool tang of October, the bustling intersection alive with honking traffic and the multinational crowds discoursing along the pavements, were a tonic to me, reviving the aura of a holiday to be enjoyed. I could afford the leisure of waiting for a bus and of not having to glance anxiously at my wristwatch. The afternoon offered a host of uptown Fifth Avenue diversions, once I'd finished with my business.

A No. 2 bus soon rumbled up to the curb. Clutching my free transfer, like the old man I was, I climbed onto the No. 2 and popped the transfer into the automated coin box at the driver's seat. Since the bus wasn't crowded, I was awarded the prize of a double window seat for my own, facing front. Usually I rode in the side seats up front behind the driver, reserved for the elderly and the handicapped, where you can't get a view of much of anything.

The No. 2 made a wrenching turn onto 26th, and, west a block, onto Madison Avenue, which was bordered by the greenery of the little city park whose name it shared. As the bus negotiated the wide turn, I could see, craning up from the window, the copper-gilded splendor of the tower that crowned the New York Life building. When I was eighteen, I'd applied at New York Life for a summer job, which I didn't get, thinking to earn some money before I set off for college in September.

As early as then, the idea of becoming a writer possessed me. Why a writer? It was the only profession I felt capable of pursuing.

The one success in my years of schooling was the stories and essays I'd got published in my high-school magazine. What other profession could I attempt—doctor, lawyer, Indian chief? No, it was strictly by default that I aspired to be a writer.

There it was, memory lane beckoning me down its shadowy, sometimes treacherous wandering paths.

Enough, enough!

I pulled my gaze from the window, straightened up in my seat. The bus trundled up Madison in the shriek and tangled skeins of traffic, and what I saw next had to do with the odyssey of where I was going and where it had begun.

I saw, in the window of my memories, the ugly interior of my old parish church of St. Thomas the Apostle, in Woodhaven, Queens, twenty-five, but more like a thousand miles away from the glittering city where, even as a boy, I'd yearned to live.

I saw that boy, troubled and unhappy, kneeling alone in the deserted church. He'd come there one afternoon from the church school next door to pray to God, as the sisters at school had taught him to do, for help in his troubles. The boy, who felt unworthy of help from God, was unable to pray. Giving up on it, and beating a hasty exit down the aisle, he'd spied, half-hidden at the rear of a side aisle, the statue of a saint that immediately had captured his attention. Saints, the sisters had told him, were our friends in heaven, our intermediaries to obtain favors from God, and with that in mind, he'd gone over, lickety-split, for a closer look at the unidentified statue.

I sank back in my seat on the bus, helpless to ward off the memories, or the problems of the book I couldn't get a handle on, that were causing me such misery. Well, she whom I regarded as *my* saint, *my* Thérèse, belonging especially to me, had more than once assisted me, or so I believed, out of other miseries, and thus I allowed myself to remember those incidents when I'd felt her presence close to me...

The article of faith was one that I'd seriously miscalculated. Brought up as a Catholic, at odds with my church, I'd left it behind me when I went away to college. Finished, done with it, the paraphernalia of holy days of obligation, the sacrifice of the Mass, the Eucharist, the sacraments, the confessional, the prayers, the nine-day novenas to the Blessed Virgin in May. No more of that nonsense for me, thanks. Over the next few years, I'd congratulated myself at having succeeded in separating myself from it. But then one day in Paris, sick in spirit and heart and body from what I'd experienced of the war, I was confronted by the startling truth that the faith, the gift of faith that I'd discarded, was still very much alive in me, undiminished, preserved intact. I might have abandoned it, but somehow, by what means I couldn't fathom, it had not abandoned me.

The cause of that truth hitting me in the face was the procession I'd stumbled upon, by chance, in the square of Notre Dame. The occasion for the procession was a mystery to me, until, hemmed in by the crowds, I deduced that it was in honor of the reliquary carried aloft with such pomp and circumstance, containing the relics of the saint whose statue had so attracted me as a boy, and who, ever since that day, had stolen in and out of my consciousness, like a favorite character from a novel or the movies.

It was as if, as the reliquary was carried past me, she had acknowledged me, with a nod and a smile, in the crowds.

If I believed in her validity as a saint of God's, it also meant that I believed, despite my removal from it, in the validity of the church and its precepts.

Not long afterward, back home again, I returned to the practice of my faith. I strove to conform my life according to my beliefs.

And in the course of the years, I acquainted myself in books with the life of St. Thérèse. As the years advanced, and my acquaintance with her deepened, she often in effect seemed to be at my side, a gentle advocate, in times of distress.

So many times, going back over the years...

It was the summer of 1956. In July, our first child, Teresa, was born. The walk-up flat in Greenwich Village where my wife and I lived, the cramped space, the flights of stairs, was no place to rear a child. So we moved to a pleasant two-bedroom apartment in Stuyvesant Town, the Met Life housing project on the Lower East Side, to which we brought home from the hospital, two years later, our second child, a son, Francis.

I was earning our income as a writer of television scripts for the Kraft Theatre, the Wednesday-night drama series broadcast on NBC. Each afternoon of that summer, I had assigned myself the mission of visiting my literary agent, to whom I owed my budding career, Phyllis Anderson, who was as well my dear and beloved friend, in New York Hospital.

Phyllis was dying of bone cancer. Radical brain surgery had failed to stop the spread of the cancer. Drugs were pumped into her, and twice a week she was wheeled into the bunker-like radiation room for treatment, but there would be no survival for her, of which she had not been informed. Her husband, Robert Anderson, the playwright, had ordained that, for her sake, she must never know she was dying. A conspiracy of well-meaning friends, visiting her bedside, perpetuated the fiction that she was getting better, day by day, and would recover to win out over the disease.

Robert spent the mornings with her, while I and other friends relieved him until he returned for the evening hours. Whatever I thought of the conspiracy, I kept it to myself. My mission was simply to cheer her up, make her laugh and reminisce about the good times together, the gay lunches at the Madison Hotel, the parties she gave for her young writers. We'd talk of the theater world that she loved and served, and she always enjoyed hearing the latest Hollywood gossip.

And, privately, my mission was to pray for her, at Mass, on a bus, a rosary hidden in my pocket, telling the beads, on the street, on my knees by the bed at night, praying that God, if nobody else, would help her to face her death and to die at peace with herself, without struggle or fear.

The difficulty with my visits, I felt certain, was that Phyllis was participating in the conspiracy. For all of her brave talk of recovery, she knew, from her worsening condition, the shocking weight loss, the constant, gnawing dull ache of pain, that she was not recovering, but the reverse.

Usually, I was alone with Phyllis, except for the in-and-out nurses, for an hour or so, before a fresh crew of friends arrived. I would draw up a chair close to her bed, keeping up a flow of talk and jokes for her amusement. She lay, rail thin, under the sheets. A pink chiffon scarf was tied over her shaved head. Her face, gazing at me, was gaunt and haggard. Her neck was encased in a harness, since the bones could not support her head. The conversation between us consisted of what was said and left unsaid.

"Look at me, Arthur, poor old skin and bones," she laughed. "The day I walk out of here, whenever that is, I'll frighten the birds off the trees."

But you'll never walk out of here. "You, Phyllis, frighten any-thing?" *You laugh, but what are you really thinking?* "The birds will flutter around you, in welcome, just like a Disney cartoon."

"The day I walk out of here, I'll go straight to Elizabeth Arden's and treat myself to a glorious make over."

"Yes, and a dazzling new wardrobe at Hattie Carnegie's." *At night, when Robert and the nurses leave, and the lights go out, what terrible visions are yours in the dark?* "We'll make a date for drinks at the good old Madison bar."

"Only if you'll let me get the tab."

Phyllis, Phyllis, I want to help you face what's to come, and not be afraid, but how can I help you with silly talk?

One afternoon, however, the talk took a different turn.

I'd always made it a practice, in any gathering, not to refer to my spiritual beliefs. The gift of faith was God's, not mine, to give. The one exception with Phyllis was a year ago, when she and Robert were to fly on vacation to Europe. She dreaded the flight, didn't trust airplanes, not for a minute, and so as a going-away gift I gave her a gold medal of St. Christopher, to tuck in her purse on the plane. Of no religious affiliation herself, the idea of medals and saints as protectors had delighted her fancy. She'd reported on her return that she'd kept the medal, not in her purse, but clasped in her hand, on the flight over and back, and that had seemed to conclude her allusion to it.

But on that one afternoon at the hospital, after a lull in the conversation, she asked: "Do you remember, Arthur, the medal you gave me, when Bob and I were flying to Europe? St. Christopher, you said, was the patron saint of travelers. Well, tell me, is there a patron saint for the sick? Or perhaps some special saint that you pray to for help?"

"Well, yes, I guess there is. Would you like me to loan her to you?"

"Yes, I rather think I would."

I'd brought her, the next day, a photograph of St. Thérèse. She held it in her emaciated hands and touched a finger to it. "Why, she's perfectly lovely, isn't she? I didn't know there were any photographs of saints."

"Thérèse didn't live that long ago. She was French, you know, from Normandy, and a writer."

"Was she, really? Here, you must pin her to the lampshade on my bed table, so I can look at her from my pillows."

I did as she'd asked. "Her being a writer, why not think of her as one of your clients? She would have made you plenty of dough."

"Yes, and I would have represented her interests like a tiger." Another lull in the conversation. "But how will I pray to her? The theater, I expect, has been my religion, but that's no help to me now, is it?'"

"If you want, I'll write you a prayer."

"Oh, would you, Arthur?" Her voice was like a child's lost in the dark. "You see, I haven't any of my own."

The prayer that I wrote on an index card for Phyllis, which she kept within reach on the bed table, read: *Little Thérèse, I give myself into your protection. Carry my love to God, and bring back his love to me. Ask the gentle Lord for everything I need. Stay close to me, Thérèse. Guard me from harm this hour, and all the hours of my life.*

Whether Phyllis had recourse to the prayer, I never learned, for I never asked. In the few months that remained for her, neither of us spoke of it again.

She was released from New York Hospital in September. Robert took her home by ambulance to their apartment in a brownstone on East 65th. She weighed seventy pounds by then and didn't speak of the day that she would walk again. When I visited one afternoon, she asked, "Why is this happening to me? What's the good of it? I can't understand why it's happening."

It tore at my innards not to have an answer to her question, one that would make sense to her. I'd wanted so much to give to Phyllis comfort, cheer, jokes, prayers, whatever, and it tore at me that I'd given her nothing.

The end was still a dragging, unsparing two months away. One night in early November, I sat hunched and mute at Phyllis's bedside in her room at St. Luke's Hospital, where she'd been taken to die.

She lay in the bed, wasted and spent, drifting into unconsciousness. Her body was ceasing to function. She was toxic, icy cold to the touch, and not within anyone's reach.

No more, no more, the conversations between us, spoken or not. At seven o'clock, I left the hospital and stood for a moment under the canopy that stretched over the entrance steps. *Was tonight goodbye to Phyllis, to what was left of her?* A thunderstorm had broken over the night sky, in slashing sheets of rain and distant growls of thunder, for which I had no raincoat or umbrella. Nothing for it but to pull up my jacket collar and make a run for the subway.

I darted out from the canopy into the sheets of rain. I didn't know my way around the Upper West Side and headed north on Morningside Drive. Across the street the hills and rocky inclines of the park were sheathed in rain. I went past a curious, round-shaped, domed building, nested behind an iron picket fence. I assumed it belonged to the sprawling Columbia University campus. I'd gone a block further up the drive when it occurred to me that the 110th St. stop of the I.R.T. was in the opposite direction. So I swung around, reversing my steps, sloshing past the curious building again. I noticed this time the sign on the plaque at the side of the double doors behind the iron fence.

Church of Notre Dame.

Wouldn't have guessed it. A light flickered dimly from within the building.

Well, where else but the cold, dank netherworld of the subway had I to go? Shivering, soaked to the skin by the rain, the church offered shelter.

Good place to sort out the tumult of one's thoughts.

I went up the steps, in through the doors and vestibule, into the church proper, and dipped a finger in the holy water font. The church was of a diminutive size, too small to accommodate a parish, so what was its function? It was dimly lit, steeped in shadows, and deserted. The sacristy lamp cast a reddish glow over the altar. A forest of candles spluttered in the racks of votive lights. It existed for prayer and worship, if nothing else.

Weary and sorrowing, soaked from the rain, hair slicked wet with it, I nudged into a rear pew and squatted there, drained of emotion. The rain dripped from me in a puddle at my feet. I made no attempt at prayer. *Pray for what?* I couldn't bring myself to pray, was the extent of it. After a while, it began to seem as if I were being sucked into a time warp, sucked back in time to another church, deserted like this one, to a boy kneeling alone in the sea of pews, who'd come to pray for God's help, but couldn't muster a prayer to ask for help.

I was that boy, of course, and now again the same sense of utter futility gripped me in a vise. All that cruel suffering pain, and what had I offered to Phyllis that was of any help or solace, *nothing, nothing…*

But, wait, didn't I know better than that?

I stumbled out of the pew and wandered up the aisle, raking a hand in my wet-slick hair, trying to sort out what it was that I believed.

We human critters, weak and venal, selfish and craven, greedy and grabbing—what one thing did we possess, worthy of giving, that was ours to give, should we but choose to give it?

To offer to others the thing of worth, above all else, in one's self, was to offer them love, which was God telling us—and was that not what I had offered, given to Phyllis, days upon days at her bedside?

I wandered about the church, distractedly, raking at my hair. In the form of a rotunda, capped high up by a dome, a colonnade of arches converted the side aisles into cloisters, masked in the shadows. If it wasn't a parish church, what was it? The decoration, the gilding of the dome, the blue velvet wall hangings were of a French elegance and restraint, it seemed to me. Yes, that was the answer. The Church of Notre Dame was, like others in the city, a national rather than a parish church, staffed by French priests, serving a congregation of French worshipers. At the suggestion of it, a sudden wild hope seized at me. I glanced around me, not finding what I sought, and went to explore one cloistered aisle, and then the side aisle under the arches across from it.

And there, facing me from the shadows, much as I'd spied her years ago, was a statue of a young nun in a black veil, a white cloak, and in her arms was a crucifix laden with roses.

It was my Thérèse, and what I'd sorted out was true. In coming each day to visit Phyllis in the hospital, I'd given her the thing of worth in me, the gift above any other, which was love.

141

And what but love had Phyllis, who was without the faith that taught it, given to me and to all of her visitors?

But was she at the last bereft of faith?

"Prayer," Thérèse had said, *"is an aspiration of the heart to God. It is a simple glance directed at heaven, it is a cry of gratitude and love in the midst of trial as well as of joy."*

Having, as she'd told me, none of her own, Phyllis had asked me for a prayer, and I had written one for her on an index card that she'd kept on her bed table. It didn't matter whether she'd said the prayer or not. In the simple act of her asking, wasn't that a prayer in itself?

I knew whereof I spoke, for once as a boy a saint had heard my prayer, though it was silent and left unsaid, and had answered it.

I reached a hand, as I did as a boy, to the base of the statue of my friend in heaven, in gratitude, and then I trooped down the aisle and out of the church.

Outside, the rain had stopped, the thunderstorm had passed, and the night sky was ablaze with stars.

Two mornings later, Phyllis died in her hospital bed at St. Luke's. She had passed beyond suffering and struggle and fear, and was somewhere else, in a place of light and peace...

The Madison Avenue bus swerved sharply, pitching me back in my seat and jolting me out of memory lane.

A girl in sweatshirt, jeans and ponytail was seated next to me, chewing gum. The bus on its journey up Madison had grown crowded. Old folks were stuffed in the side seats behind the driver, my usual turf. With a screech and grinding of brakes, we pulled to a stop at 42nd.

The time was fast approaching, in more ways that one, for the finish of my particular journey.

Moments later, I got off at Madison and 50th. Tired and spent from my trip down memory lane, to say nothing of two struggling years at the typewriter, I felt confused, befuddled for an instant, as to where I was or should be headed.

Across the avenue rose the spires of St. Patrick's Cathedral. Into the bronze doors of 50th St., crowds were streaming, telling me where and for what I was bound. A year ago in March, at the invitation of the Friends of St. Thérèse, I'd attended a special Mass of Cardinal O'Connor's. The occasion was to celebrate the naming of my saint by John Paul II as a doctor of the church, only the third woman, along with Teresa of Avila and Catherine of Sienna, to be thus honored.

Today was to be a homage to her.

The traffic light favored me with a flash of red. With the caution of an old duffer, I got to the other side of Madison. That little book of hers, that she'd never intended to write, what riches it had wrought in the world! And I, would I never get a handle on the book I was attempting of her life?

At the 50th St. entrance, clutching onto the handrail, I went toiling up the steps. Years and years of smoking cigarettes had spelled emphysema for me. Damaged lungs. A shortness of breath, loss of energy that severely restricted my physical activities. It was often touch and go, in the last months of work on the book, as to which would prevail, it or my disability.

Well, never mind, I'd made it to St. Patrick's today, just as I'd hoped.

In through the great bronze doors I went, unprepared for what greeted me. The Mass wasn't until four o'clock, but already, almost an hour earlier, the vast cathedral was filled with people by the thousands, and more were streaming through the doors.

I hung back in the entry, concerned that I wouldn't be able to do what I'd come for. Crowds were moving slowing, inch by inch, down the aisles. Up front, directly below the main altar, a reliquary in the shape of a casket was raised on a platform above the crowds. It had arrived yesterday in New York from Brazil and would depart tomorrow on the next stop of a world tour. Fifty-four years ago, in the crowded square at Notre Dame in Paris, the relics had been carried passed me in procession, on a day that would change my life forever.

And here on this day, again, was I in the presence of my saint, my Thérèse, as for a long while I had sought to be close to her in spirit.

LOVE!

What else had brought all of us thousands to the cathedral, but that? How wisely did Thérèse teach us the way of love in her book—the Little Way of trust in God and seeking to do his will for us. "I intend to be very busy in Heaven, helping out down here below," she said, as she lay dying on a cross of suffering, in imitation, her whole life, of Jesus. It would seem, from the thousands gathered here today, and the hundreds of thousands who would pay homage to her relics on the tour, that her deathbed wishes had been fulfilled.

The crowds pushed slowly down the aisles toward the main altar. Would my breath turn ragged and gasping, should I attempt the journey, obliging me to drop out before I'd reached my goal?

I'd never get another chance at it. I sighed, and another quote from my saint slipped into my mind: *"I've always gone where I've wanted to go."* So then, borrowing her sentiment, I made use of it myself.

Stepping from the entry, I joined the slow, surging crowd in the side aisle nearest me, the last instead of the first, as Thérèse would want of me. Inch by inch, at a snail's pace, but breathing steadily, I approached the main altar. Whether the reliquary on the platform was the one carried past me at Notre Dame, I could not say, as I inched closer to it. Flowers were scattered over it and the platform, flowers slipping in a whoosh to the marble floor.

How extraordinary, this tribute to a saint, all these thousands, come from distances to touch a hand to the reliquary, in a gesture of love. Each would have a tale to tell of a prayer answered, a job won, the rent paid, a child's illness cured. To each of these thousands she was "my" Thérèse, belonging to each and every one of us.

At last I stood below the reliquary on the platform. If I'd expected, as I reached up a hand to touch it, a surge of emotion, I felt instead strangely empty and drained. Would I ever be able to do justice to her in my book and not despoil it with faults? As I turned away from the flower-strewn platform—how alike it was to the square that day of Notre Dame—I glimpsed on the platform a silver vase of long-stemmed red roses, and tears stung my eyes. Ah, the splendor of the rose was not for Thérèse. No, a little white flower, plucked from a garden wall, spoke for who she was.

And the flower that she had unpetalled, out of love of Jesus, in her suffering and death, was herself.

By then, as four o'clock drew near, I went searching for a seat in the full-up pews. I was fairly worn out and spent. Let me confess that during the Mass that was celebrated, I dozed off, head nodding, half asleep. In that nether state of consciousness, the image of the little white flower materialized before me, and somehow I knew that I wasn't on the wrong track with my book and must write the story of Thérèse as I perceived it, from my own perspective.

She was the saint who loved us.

After the Mass had concluded, I crossed over Fifth Avenue to the bus stop at the corner. Too worn out, I gave up any idea of a treat at Burger Heaven. As a No. 3 bus rolled up, I settled for the ride home. I climbed aboard and didn't worry about getting a window seat.

Home, after all, wasn't so far away.